The Discovery
Tarot Path

The Discovery Tarot Path

· · · · · · ·

A New Model for Self-Reading
with the Rider-Waite-Smith Deck

STEPHANIE LEON NEAL

TURNING
S T O N E
P R E S S

Table of Contents

This book is dedicated to the woman who lovingly taught me the Tarot in 1970, my beloved mother-in-law, Margaret Ruth Neal.

"Archetypes resemble the beds of rivers: dried up because the water has deserted them, though it may return at any time. An archetype is something like an old watercourse along which the water of life flowed for a time, digging a deep channel for itself. The longer it flowed the deeper the channel, and the more likely it is that sooner or later the water will return."

—Carl Jung

Introduction

Welcome to the Discovery Tarot Path. This path is designed to assist individuals in seeking guidance through interpretation of the Rider-Waite-Smith (RWS) Tarot deck. Using this time-honored and beloved deck, individuals will learn how to easily read their own cards and discover powerful answers to life's questions. This book offers a new method of reading the Tarot in order to cultivate personal happiness and well-being.

Through this new method, experienced Tarot readers and nonexperienced readers alike may inform their future. As a spiritual counselor and teacher for over four decades, I have discovered a way of reading the Tarot through what I call "keys," explained later in this book, which are an infinitely invaluable tool to help individuals find their own answers as they regain their personal power and inner sovereignty. If you do not already own an original style Rider-Waite-Smith Tarot deck, you will need to acquire one in order to complete the exercises and studies found in this book. This popular deck can be easily found in many bookstores, metaphysical supply stores, and online.

Experienced Tarot readers may already know that the Tarot can be read in many ways and with many different approaches. For our purposes, however, we are only going to focus on one of the basic ways to read the Tarot: self-reading, or a reading that you do for yourself and not for another person. Many people have difficulty reading their own cards, but this book will instruct you how to easily perform this skill. In fact, the Discovery Tarot Path requires you to read your own cards because the solutions found there must come from your own inner wisdom; they are after all the solutions to your own challenges— not anyone else's. Reading in this way is simple and straightforward, but it does require trusting and believing in yourself. There is no room for second-guessing in this path; only believing. There are no wrong answers when you are interpreting the cards with this method. In the same way that physical keys open physical doors, the Tarot keys will open the doors to inner wisdom and knowledge; the more you read your cards for yourself, the wider these doors open.

You and the Universe are continually writing your personal story, but the Discovery Tarot Path can help you identify the obstacles that consistently hound you and help reveal options that can help you move beyond fear, lack, self-doubt, low self-esteem, or shame. The Tarot tells a story bigger than time and space, and the Discovery Tarot Path helps you interpret that story in order to help you, and planet Earth, take the next evolutionary leap.

The Tarot Discovery Path is truly a magical journey to your inner power. It is ultimately a guide for helping us to evolve, see our connections, and learn how to take care of our part on this planet, and our place within this colossal growing existence.

≈ 1 ≈

What Is the Tarot?

*Creative ideas, in my opinion, show their value
in that, like keys, they help to "unlock" hitherto
unintelligible connections of facts and thus enable
man to penetrate deeper into the mystery of life.*

—M. L. von Franz

As we step into the journey of learning the Discovery Tarot Path, I advise that you begin to think of the Tarot as a book about everything, because that is what it is. As you move through your life, read the Tarot as though it is *your* story.

To describe what the Tarot is, it helps to survey the scant history scholars have uncovered regarding the cards up to this point of time. We only have theories regarding the Tarot's inception and how the deck arrived in Europe. Many believe that the deck holds the story of humankind and its process; some believe the cards' visuals give wisdom through oracular power. The Tarot is a mirror that reflects what you are at any given moment as well as informs you about your future and clarifies your past. The Tarot prefers to be utilized for your personal growth so you may "Know Thy Self." It is a compendium of the Mystery traditions throughout time, including astrology, Kabbalah, Alchemy, Egyptian thought, numerology, Hermetic philosophy, Christianity, Neo-Platonic philosophy, the Hermetic Order, and the Golden Dawn. The cards have been further influenced by Eastern and Western philosophies, Sufism, Byzantine literati, and French royalty, etc. There are gaping holes in our knowledge of the Tarot's origins. The how and where are nowhere to be found at this point, yet the cards remain influenced greatly by a large part of the world. Plus the Tarot is still growing and collects more interpretations and influences each passing year.

The earliest mention of the cards was in 1367 in the city of Bern, Switzerland, in a proclamation banning the use of cards for gambling purposes. The ban did not mention divination, but it did state that these cards were "picture books of the devil."

A few years later in 1376 there was another proclamation in Florence speaking against using cards for gambling, yet it also did not mention divination. The Minor Arcana at this time were called *Nahipi* or *Naibbe*. In 1377 the Minor Arcana's earliest descriptions were written by Frater Johannes von Rheinfelden. The earliest known Tarot deck only consists of the Minor Arcana named the "Hunting Deck" of Stuttgard, c. 1420. The oldest description of all twenty-two cards was discussed or at least named in an anonymous sermon written by a Dominican friar dated between 1450 and 1480 discouraging people from playing dice and playing games; in English the sermon was called "Sermon of games with dice."

The earliest decks that consisted of both the Minor (the suits) and Major (the named cards, or "Trumps") Arcana were the Visconti-Sforza decks created for the Duke of Milan circa 1440 for an event he was hosting.

These were referred to as "triumph" or *Trionfi* cards, referencing a game played with them in Italy. The Duke of Milan's deck held four suits, including numerals one through ten, all four court cards within each suit, and twenty-two scenes that belonged to no suit. The first time the Tarot was mentioned in writing was in 1442, which is the earliest recorded account naming every card. Trionfi decks are first mentioned in the D' Este court of Ferrara's ledger books in 1442.

The cards were eventually called *Tarocchi*, which is an Italian version of the word *Tarot*. The earliest painted decks are the Cary-Yale, Este, Charles VI, and Visconti decks. The oldest literary reference is the Steele Manuscript.

Once the cards appeared in Italy it took over 350 years for someone to add further information about the Tarot, and that was Antoine Court de Gebelin, who promoted the idea that the Tarot deck was created in ancient Egypt. Shortly after this information was published, it was "Etteilla," who created his own deck using the Egyptian story called the *Book of Thoth*, for his influence, yet it is unclear that Etteilla was the first to create a deck based on the *Book of Thoth* or that he was the first to alter the deck.

As decades passed, more cultures, philosophies, and religions added, subtracted, or altered the symbols, just enough, to reflect their belief systems.

Tarot is a living thing desiring to communicate with humans, as all things desire to communicate with us and it is our own subconscious desire to communicate with them. The Tarot is a tool to help you receive messages from your higher-self, the part of you that can hear the voice of Divine guidance.

Tarot is what you think it is. Like everything in life, you see through your world view, hopefully with an open mind and an open heart, when communing with the Tarot. The Tarot holds secrets of the universe and humankind while explaining how spiritual growth and ascension are in your hands using visuals.

Tarot is a microcosm of the universe and the journey of humans portrayed through beautiful symbolism. Tarot is a method of assessing your life and its influences. The Tarot is a picture book filled with wisdom that answers every question on Earth related to the human condition representing both her story and his story. This wise Oracle helps you to ascend to new dimensions and awaken in your time, manner, and place through the Major Arcana. Every question is answered within every card because it is we who hold every answer within ourselves. The Tarot is a faithful mirror that reflects us and our journey.

There is no wrong or right way for reading the Tarot even though there are a few folks that think there is only one way to shuffle, lay out a spread, select a card, and read the cards. Since they think there is only one way, then by all means continue to enjoy the cards the way you were instructed. No harm done.

For the rest of us please explore and enjoy utilizing different approaches until you find a few that are comfortable for your sensibilities.

The Basic Mechanics

The Tarot normally contains seventy-eight cards divided into two groups: the Major Arcana and Minor Arcana. The word *Arcana* is Latin for "secrets" and "mysteries." Thus the Major Arcana is the "Greater Mysteries" and the Minor Arcana are the "Lesser Mysteries."

The Minor Arcana are further divided into four suits: Cups, Pentacles, Swords, and Wands. Each suit contains ten cards numbered 1–10 and four Court cards: Page, Knight, Queen, and King. The Minor Arcana in total consist of fifty-six cards, which include fourteen cards per suit.

The Minor cards can be called any of the following names:

Pentacles = Coins, Disks, Rings, or Diamonds

Cups = Chalices or Hearts

Wands – Batons, Staves, or Clubs

Swords = Spades in playing cards

The Minor Arcana reflect an individual's everyday life and influences affecting their missions.

The Major Arcana consist of twenty-two cards numbered 0–21. In current decks the Fool card (0) is first, while some of the older decks have the Fool card following after the World card (21). Additionally, there are a few earlier decks where the Fool shows up between the last two cards of the Major Arcana, between 20 and 21. The Major Arcana reflect an individual's spiritual life or the bigger picture regarding your spiritual growth. The Major Arcana also reveal a story of humankind's stages of ascension and process.

The Tarot retrieves guidance for your life in the present while uncovering hidden hindrances from the past that may be affecting your present and future. In essence, the Tarot is a key that opens the door to an Oracle, a wise counselor, or a wise sage residing in you we call our higher-self. If you have difficulty believing this, then just read what the symbols are revealing to you through your belief system.

How the Tarot Works

Cartomancy is the practice of utilizing any cards for telling the future. On the surface it seems the Tarot is just a deck of cards created to play the Italian card game called Tarocchi mentioned earlier. But how can these cards be used to find answers to questions?

Think of the Tarot as a tool that helps you communicate with your unconscious. Then as you interpret the scene on the card, you are freeing your mind to flow easily as you just say what you think you see. You are taking an open-ended scene and then telling a story for the querent, seeker, or you.

The Tarot is not static; it is always expanding and changing, as it should. The Tarot is utilized by most for divination purposes so individuals may prepare, avoid, or change the situation they now find themselves. Others may wish to enter into the Tarot as a lifelong path, studying the symbol meanings, learning how to become a problem solver, and learning how to live life to its fullest. The Tarot is a path to Deity, reality, and spirituality … or you may just enjoy learning how to get through each day successfully; whatever success means to you.

The Tarot depicts what humans walk through as they reach spiritual ascension, focusing on the Source of all which encompasses all. If we focus on Source, we know we are part of the all and that through our highest self we can develop our psychic awareness of universality versus individuality. To say it another way, if you believe you work through Deity and are part of Deity, then you can see through your psychic eyes by looking at a symbol and allowing Deity to speak to you through your interpretation of that symbol. Allow yourself to rest in stillness as you see through Deity's eyes. Believe in yourself and believe that you are part of Source—thus all wisdom opens to you, and flows through you like a hollow bone.

A Basic Reading

The Tarot's General Instructions

The following information is how traditional spreads are read. When first working with the Tarot, spend time with each card by identifying all the symbols within each card. Ask yourself, What does this card say to me? How does this card make me feel? With what do I associate this card? Start with just one-card readings. Do not overcomplicate the interpretation. If you are a beginner and want to read the Tarot for others or yourself, here are the basics:

A Traditional Reading Has the Following Components and Actions

- A friendly atmosphere.

- A deck of cards you enjoy reading. This book focuses on the Rider-Waite-Smith deck, but there are many decks out there.

- Opening with prayer. Call forth Spirit to bless the cards and the reading in any way you prefer. I personally place my hand over the cards and say silently, "I open your Divine energy and I bless you. Show me only the truth, not the person's hopes or fears unless it is important to know at this time."

- Cleansing the cards by shuffling them four times or until they feel "right" or "ready" clears all energies off the cards so the querent has a clean slate. During this process, I continue praying silently, "I now speak to Deity, my higher-self and all that is sacred, please give lighted guidance to this seeker. Open her awareness; open my awareness to receive what she needs within this eternal moment through this deck that is now attuned to her."

- Determining a question. If you cannot think of a specific question, you can ask, "What do I need to know at this time?"

- Asking the question and shuffling. The querent thinks of the question as she shuffles the cards (though some readers prefer to shuffle the cards themselves while the querent concentrates on her question). There are several ways to shuffle the cards: Overhand shuffling, riffle shuffling, and the Cauldron Dump Method: Dump the cards on the table, then move them around the table, then select your cards.

- Cutting the deck. The querent cuts the deck in two or three piles with the left hand; the left hand represents spirituality and the Goddess's guidance. I have seen readings where the reader cuts the cards, but I personally let the querent cut the cards.

- Laying out the spread. The reader selects a Tarot spread, which is the pattern that the cards take on the table. An example of this is the Celtic cross pattern; it is an equal-armed cross and a straight staff on the cross's right side. (Yet I have seen the cards laid out many different ways for the Celtic cross.) The querent should know a few Tarot spreads or at least have a little chart of the spread pattern and what each position represents. There are hundreds of Tarot spreads, yet most Tarot readers enjoy using the Celtic Cross spread to divine the cards; thus I will add the general steps to read this popular spread. A spread predetermines how you lay the Tarot cards on a flat surface, how many cards are in play, and that each position represents a specific meaning. Using most spreads, the reader has more information to interpret, through the card positions in the spread; i.e., each card as a single unit or the cards can be read together as one unit, and where each card lands in a particular spread adds another layer to the meaning of the cards. Each position in a spread represents a pre-established meaning. An example of this is the three-card spread; the first card on the left depicts the past, the middle card position depicts the present, and the last card on the right shows the outcome or future. (There are several types of three-card spreads.)

Some readers use a significator card when reading, and some spreads call for a significator card. This means one card in the spread is selected or an additional card is selected ahead of time to represent the significator/querent.

A note about reversals: The Discovery Tarot Path does not typically consider reversals, which are cards that are upside down. There are a lot of resources on how to read "reversed" cards, but for this method we will focus on the upright images only.

- Turning the cards. After the reader has laid her spread out, it is time to turn the cards. Some turn all the cards over as they lay them on the table while others turn them over one at a time as they discuss the reading. For some readers the way they turn the cards is important to them. Some examples of this is some will only turn the cards from the left over, while others will flip each card over from the right side, or some will turn each card over from the bottom up or top down. It all depends on how you were trained.

- Reading and interpreting. Each card has a mutable meaning depending on the question. The reader receives the meaning from her/his higher-self, the portion of every being that is completely connected to Divine Source of the Soul.

Every card holds several symbols that together can convey both an issue and one or more solutions to that issue. The most difficult task for some individuals is to interpret the solution through the symbols that are displayed on the card. I always begin by first identifying what I am actually seeing on the card: What is the scene? Who is in the scene? What are they doing? What result will this scene have?

This is where you have to really look at the card and see the symbols themselves, not other people's interpretations, but what is really there in front of your eyes, because a symbol will take on a different meaning for everyone. What we want to find in each card is a solution that works specifically for you for your specific problem in your specific life; and the only person who can know if a solution or meaning resonates with you is you. More examples are presented in later chapters.

The Discovery Tarot Path Reading Method

The Discovery Tarot Path reading involves similar steps to the outline above, but it is different from reading the Tarot for another individual because your focus is solely on solving your own issues or learning how to grow spiritually.

When you read for yourself, you will want to write down your question before you start shuffling and selecting your key to form a spread. You may want to keep your spread out on a table for days so you can just sit with it and ponder solutions, because sometimes the answers do not appear in one day.

For the work in this book, we will us the Rider-Waite-Smith deck. This deck was drawn by the illustrator Pamela Colman Smith from instructions by Dr. A. E. Waite and published by the Rider Company in 1909, along with A. E. Waite's popular book *The Pictorial Key to the Tarot*, which followed in 1911. You may have a favorite Tarot deck already, and it is a good idea to use your favorite deck alongside the Rider-Waite-Smith deck at the same time as a comparison. Whenever the Rider-Waite-Smith deck is used, always keep in mind the Tarot de Marseille deck, because Waite and Smith based their deck on the Marseille deck and they made many changes in the Major Arcana and added pictures to the Minor Arcana pips, which was only the second time pictures were added to the suits' pips (Minor Arcana); the Sola-Busca Tarot deck created in the late 1400s added illustrations to pip cards.

Taking Care of Your Deck

Simply store your deck away in a protective bag, a wooden or tin box, or wrap the deck in a scarf. It is always good form to bless the cards and space you will be using when working with the Tarot. Keep them in a cool, dry place and shuffle them to cleanse them before and after each use.

Some Other Useful Terminology Before We Begin

The Suits' Hierarchy: Wands, Pentacles, Cups, and Swords.

Reader: The person interpreting the cards.

Querent: Also called the seeker, this is the person asking the question. In the Discovery Tarot Path, you are the querent as well as the reader since you are reading for yourself.

Crossings: A crossing is anything that makes a cross on the card's rendering. The meaning of a crossing is from spirit to matter and matter into spirit. They are the space between the worlds. Every time you identify one of these "crossings," it means that your manifestation is in your own hands, so act accordingly. The place between the realms reminds us that we have everything to manifest what is needed to become more evolved or less evolved. In the Major Arcana, crossings may be seen in The Hanged Man (12) and The World (21). In the Minor Arcana a few are the Two of Swords, Four of Cups, and Nine of Cups.

Keys: Keys are symbols that repeat themselves throughout the deck or open a storyline. Examples of keys would be a crossing, roses, paths, or feathers, to name a few. Keys will be discussed in greater detail later in the book.

Spreads

Here are a few common Tarot spreads to start with:

Celtic Cross Spread

The Celtic Cross is an equaled-armed cross, which is the Solar Cross of the four Directions, four Elements, four Quarters, and four Guardians of physical existence. The Celtic Cross is a very popular spread and there are many different ways of interpreting the positions of each card. One way is below.

This illustration shows how to lay the spread out and what each position means:

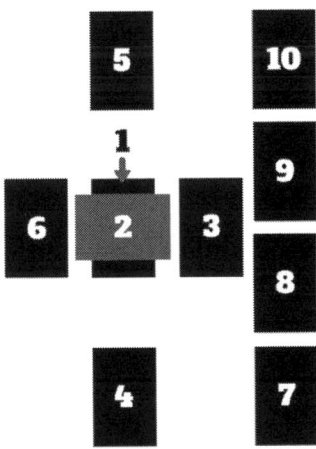

Card 0   Some individuals use a 0 position card placed under the first card. This is called the Significator card, and it represents the querent.

Card 1   **The Present:** Also called the covering card. This position represents where you are currently. The first card represents the basic energy of the querent's question and the querent's state of mind.

Card 2   **The Challenge:** Also called the crossing card. This position represents potential challenges.

Card 3   **The Past:** This position represents the past and situations that have led to the issue. Also this position represents events that caused the present situation and some indication of how the challenge came to be.

Card 4   **The Future:** Also called the crown card. This position represents where to focus for the future.

Card 5   **Past influences:** This position represents the querent's strengths and the best outcome for the querent's goals and aspirations. This is what the querent is working on consciously to resolve the issue.

Card 6   **Near Future:** This position represents what is likely to occur within the next few weeks or even months.

Card 7   **Advice:** Also called the personal card. This position represents suggested approaches to the issue.

Card 8   **External Influences:** Also called the environ-mental card. This position represents what the querent needs to know at this time. The exter-nal influences are revealed here.

Card 9   **Hopes and/or Fears:** Also called the psy-chological card. This position represents the querent's hopes and fears. It helps to draw a second card for clarification for this card if needed.

Card 10   **Final Outcome:** This position represents the potential future. If the outcome card is not a desirable outcome, the future is always in the querent's hands and can make the necessary changes to change the future.

Three more cards may be drawn, to gain more information.

Past, Present, and Future Spread

A very useful, straightforward three-card spread.

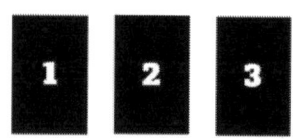

Card 1   Represents the past.

Card 2   Represents the present.

Card 3   Represents the future.

Ocean Spread

My personal favorite spread is the ocean spread. I enjoy it because the visual layout is more connective to the querent.

The ocean spread is set up with three horizontal rows as follows:

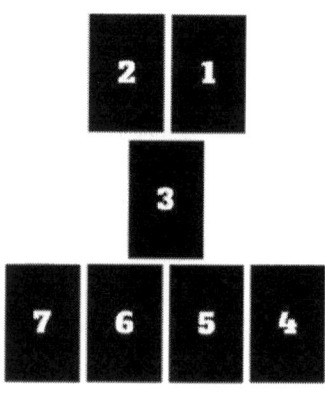

The top row represents above the water's surface: These are the things or individuals openly influencing you or the situation.

The middle row is on the water's surface: This is what is currently happening. This card also symbolizes the outcome.

The bottom row is beneath the water's surface: This is what is beneath the surface and hidden influences.

Each row is read as a complete sentence.

Success Spread

2	3	4	5	6	7	8
			1			

Card 1   Represents the querent.

Card 2   What is a barrier?

Card 3   What is your fear?

Card 4   What needs to be released?

Card 5   The time and activities devoted to your goals and aspirations.

Card 6   What you know and are applying to your life.

Card 7   Where is your hope?

Card 8   Outcome.

Interpreting the Cards

Each Tarot card contains several symbols. The most difficult task for some individuals is to interpret the solution through the symbols that are displayed on the card.

What we want to find in each card is a solution that works specifically for you for your specific problem in your specific life; and the only person who can know if a solution or meaning resonates with you is you. So as you look at a Tarot card and its symbols, such as a bird or the ocean, etc., ask yourself, "What does a flying bird mean *to me*, what does ocean mean *to me?*" Then trust that Deity will help you interpret the symbol on the card.

When you first look at a card, what are the symbols that make themselves obvious to you? Focus on the first two or three symbols that stand out to you; it is very rare that Spirit leads you to discuss every single symbol on the card unless you are studying the Major Arcana.

Here is a great example for reading a single card:

1. Consider where the card is on the Tarot card spread.

2. What story is the scene telling?

As an example, let's apply this to the Five of Swords:

> This card depicts a man holding three swords while standing next to two swords lying on the ground and two men walking away from him. At first blush it looks like the man holding the three swords is the victor over the two dejected men walking away. However, there are many ways to interpret this scene:

- The man holding the swords could have taken them from the other two men walking away from him.

- The man holding the swords could be trying to pick up the swords as he is calling to the men for help, but they are not interested in helping or they do not hear him.

- It may be that the two men were fighting, and he took the swords away from them and told them to cool off and lay down their arms.

- Or perhaps it was kids playing with things they were not supposed to play with and the father said, "Don't you make me come over there."

- Or maybe he looks satisfied because he just completed a lesson with two novices.

- Or he is walking home from work and the other two men are just strangers he is passing by.

- Or maybe the two men sold this man swords.

- Or he may be the one selling swords and can't find the voice to make a sale.

3. In addition to what's happening in the scene on the card, do the number of items in the card, or the card number itself, speak to you? Numerals count as symbols and thus you can bring numerology into the reading.

4. Another way to read the cards is to read all the cards as if in a sentence or story line, then tell the story.

When reading a spread, always consider whether you are informing the querent of the *best* outcome or the *most likely* outcome? It may be that the cards are pointing out that the issue may be remedied but not in the way the querent may prefer.

Of course there are many ways to interpret cards. If you feel more comfortable reading the book the author wrote to go along with the cards, that is fine too.

Individual Card Meanings

I have collected these meanings over the decades by jotting them down in a journal when reading the cards for myself, for others, or when my mother-in-law was teaching me.

Remember one may interpret the Tarot through pure intuition, by focusing on a single element like astrology, or by reading the cards through the lens of a belief system such as the Kabbalah or Hermitic thought. The Discovery Tarot Path is one of many approaches to the Tarot.

Once we have looked at each card's individual meaning, we will move on to explain how we interpret the Keys.

MINOR ARCANA

The Minor Arcana convey the practical everyday issues of life as represented by the general population. In medieval times the general population was divided into four categories, and as such so are the Minor Arcana. The four suits are the industrial and businessmen represented by pentacles/coins; politicians, scholars, statesmen, and clergy represented by cups; blue collar workers represented by clubs; military and nobility represented by swords. In the following section you will find possible meanings for each card in the Minor Arcana. The reason why there are so many meanings is that every culture and age has added their own world-view interpretation to every symbol. You may gain even more insight by using numerology, astrology, or adding other interpretive elements to see how this works for you.

THE SUIT OF CUPS

Themes in the Suit of Cups:
The West • Hearts • Water • Consciousness •
Emotions • Reactions • Change • Love • Healing •
Evening • Middle Age • Female

ACE OF CUPS

Consciousness

Intuition

Spirituality

Personal relationships

Emotion in its purest form

Regeneration

Expression through the senses

Overflowing abundance/ peace/emotion

Communicating with openness

Following your heart

TWO OF CUPS

Love

Equal partnership

Equality

Marriage

Change

Good health or the process
of healing

Living life on a public stage

Strong communication

Inspiration

THREE OF CUPS

Abundance
Teamwork
Harvest
Autumn
Living life to the fullest

Everyone has different gifts
Celebrating
    accomplishments
Community leaders
Emotional riches

FOUR OF CUPS

Luxury

The answers are in front of you

Pondering

Taking a time-out

Isolation

Unhappiness

Not recognizing the blessings in life

Doubt

Dealing with naysayers

Nothing is enough

Not being aware of the situation at hand

FIVE OF CUPS

Disappointment

Trying again

Identifying poison in
your life

Emotional manipulation

Senseless loss

Lingering gloom

Returning home

Taking what is yours

Not throwing the good out
with the poison

Remembering what you
have and what you know

SIX OF CUPS

Pleasure

Generosity

New friend

Gift from an admirer

New surroundings

New opportunities

Possible inheritance

Living in the past

Return to an old job

A past life bond is
  recognized

Innocence

Connecting with others
  brings strength

Gift-giving

Learning how to receive

SEVEN OF CUPS

Selecting as many goals as you like

Overwhelmed

Lots of options

Illusory success

Castles-in-the-sky thinking

Brainstorming

Fear of failure

Something is too good to be true

Identifying the poison in your life

Coming out of the shadows you cast

EIGHT OF CUPS

Indolence

Leaving to study further

Taking a break

Something is missing

River runs dry

Something new

Leaving a dream

Walking away from the drama

Giving up

Discovering something was not a healthy influence

Starting fresh

Heeding the call

Bravery

Coming to the end of the line

NINE OF CUPS

Happiness

Advantage

Physicality

Satisfaction

Opening to new ideas

Loyalty

Abundance

Time to take a spiritual
  journey

Liberty

A good future is assured

Desires will be fulfilled

TEN OF CUPS

Family

Good partner

Lessons learned through
family

A full heart

Blessings

True love

Satisfaction

Security

Thanksgiving

Trust

A feeling of arrival

Deep connection

Working together creates a
powerful force

PAGE OF CUPS

Birth of a child

Good news

An invitation

Identifying something out of place

Feeling like a fish out of water

A person who is:
    Imaginative, Optimistic, Trusting, Playful, Accommodating, Artistic, Compassionate, Understanding, Living their lives on stage,

Does the plan affect their artistic sensibilities

KNIGHT OF CUPS

Promising proposal or
collaboration

Broadening one's horizons
through a friend

New philosophy

Time to embrace the unseen
energies found under the
surface

Reciprocated love

A person who is:
Diplomatic, Artistic,
Considerate, Imaginative,
Loyal

QUEEN OF CUPS

A person who is: Fair,
  Compassionate, Loyal,
  Generous, Encouraging
  of others, Honest, Able
  to utilize emotion for
  manifestation, Fully
  devoted to the sea's
  mysteries

KING OF CUPS

Travel
Influence

A person who is: Fair,
Responsible, Deliberate,
Fully invested in the
sea's lessons, Creative,
Intelligent, A man of
business/law/clergy

THE SUIT OF PENTACLES

(Also commonly called Disks or Coins)

Themes in the Suit of Pentacles:

The North • Diamonds • Earth • Physical

External Reality • Finances • Creativity • Sensation

Material concerns • Midnight • Old Age • Female

ACE OF PENTACLES

The beginning of
 manifestation

Internal and external
 physical awareness

Richness found through
 many natural avenues

Organization

Material positions come easy

Trust your natural instincts

Help is on the way

Perfect contentment

Triumph over hardship

Internal success

TWO OF PENTACLES

Balance

Too busy to see the storm approaching

Balanced change

Perpetual motion

Balancing the bills

Dancing through harsh times

The storm is but a moment compared to eternity

Too many irons in the fire

Risky venture

Timing

Juggling resources

Uncanny instinct

THREE OF PENTACLES

Teamwork

Skill

Marketable idea

Art/Craft

Quality work

Rechecking the task/plan

Following up

Communicating what
   you need

Pleasant work environment

Asking: Is everyone on the
   same page?

Instructions

Following the map

Being aware of details

Asking: Is this a good idea?

FOUR OF PENTACLES

Power

Holding on to material
items or an inheritance

Holding on to material
things too tightly

Time to consider letting
a few things go to
make room for new
opportunities

Withholding something

Becoming stingy

Control

Knowing your limits

FIVE OF PENTACLES

Worry
Help is at hand
Asking for help
Health issues
Being aware that help
is near

Asking: do you rely on
something or someone as
a "crutch?"
Being unprepared
Being helpless yet still
having the courage and
strength to move forward
Wounded

SIX OF PENTACLES

Success

Giving/Generosity

Balance

Being aware of others' needs

Learning how to receive

Sharing from abundance

Charity

Requesting help

Investing in others is
    investing in the future

Rescuer

Fairness

SEVEN OF PENTACLES

Self-reflection

Broadening your worldview

A diligent worker

Saving your money

Wishing money grew
on trees

Taking a break

Opportunity found through
networking

Counting chickens before
they hatch

EIGHT OF PENTACLES

Prudence

Diligence

Responsibility

Focus

Self-motivatation

Paying attention to detail

Seeing issues from many
  perspectives

Using the right tools for the
  right task

Hammering out the details

Perfectionism

Independent projects

Gain won through
  hard work

NINE OF PENTACLES

Self-reliance

Celebrating the lushness of
nature

Exploration

Work that will last for
generations

Leadership

Wealth

Training

Recognition

Showcasing your abilities

Independence

TEN OF PENTACLES

Entering the gate of a new experience

Wealth

Asking for help from an Elder

Giving unconditional love

Trusted companions

Family

Inheritance

Legacy

Archives

PAGE OF PENTACLES

Solid progress
Keeping your eye on
 the prize
Perseverance

A person who is: Great
at business, Focused,
Enthusiastic, Reliable,
Dependable, Practical, An
honest, responsible, hard
worker, Disciplined, A
financial consultant, Has
incredible stamina

KNIGHT OF PENTACLES

Strong Earth element
Foundations
Slow and steady progress
Receiving money from
  several sources

A person who is: Driven,
  Self-Reliant, Focused
  on the greater good,
  Enduring, Practical,
  Sturdy, Faithful

QUEEN OF PENTACLES

Wealth of knowledge
Earth Mother
Fertility
Abundance

A person who is:
Independent, Self-made,
Generous, Productive,
Effective, A CEO,
Hardworking

KING OF PENTACLES

Knowing your worth
Good health
More organization is needed

A person who is: A Provider, Good with money, Practical, Confident, Stable, Hardworking, A maverick, Able to sweep you off your feet and take charge

THE SUIT OF SWORDS

Themes in the Suit of Swords:
East • Air • Mental • Beliefs • Attitudes • Intellect
Important Individuals • Possible Conflict • Thought
Dawn • Childhood • Male • Military • Sharp words

ACE OF SWORDS

Mental clarity
Visionary
Strength
Originality
Creative thinker
Innovative thinker
Dreams actualized
Taking a stand

Thoughts become
 crystal clear
This is your time
Receptive mind
Philosophy
This is time for triumph
 and new beginnings

TWO OF SWORDS

Peace

Initiation

Reflection

Objective thinking

Equilibrium between two
opposing forces

Weighing decisions
before acting

Truth revealed

Reasoned judgement

Moment of decision

Delay

Can't see all the facts

Not ready for a relationship

Stubbornness

THREE OF SWORDS

Sorrow

Stormy relationships

Three important individuals

Being attacked in some way

Heartbreak

Death

Disappointment

Major surgery

Depression

Betrayal

Inner or outer conflict

Sabotage

Bad news

Slander

Despair

FOUR OF SWORDS

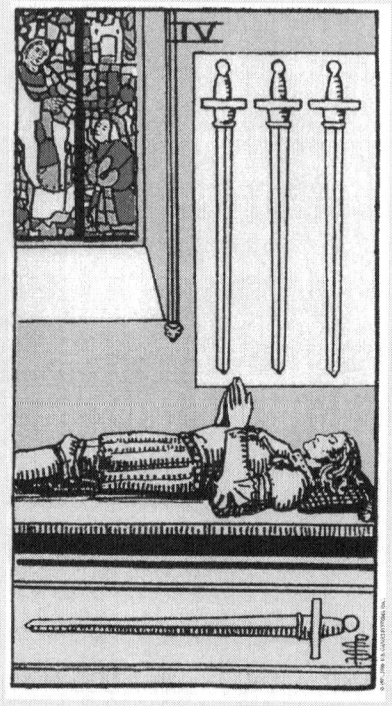

Truce	Thoughts that cause one to become frozen
Rest	
Silence	Time for new dreams and philosophy
Waiting	
Recovery	Need a break from the mind
Overworked	Meditation
Isolation	Balance
Vigil	Reflections
	Death of a thing or idea

FIVE OF SWORDS

Defeat, or victory but at
  a cost

Arrogant

Harsh competition

In-fighting

Crushing the ego

Assert dominance

Enemies acting like friends

Empty victory

Hard-headed

Others coming against you

Fear of defeat

SIX OF SWORDS

Science

Escape

Relief

Possible journey

Smooth waters

Sorrow is diminishing

Harmony will return

Safe travels

Time to leave an unhealthy situation or activity

Send another qualified person in your stead

Be aware of your surroundings

SEVEN OF SWORDS

Futility

Trickery

Thievery

Quietly walk away

Someone is removing important people in your life through manipulation

Discernment

Keep your cards close to your chest

Keeping a secret

Deceit

Running away

Be careful what you put into writing

Taking a risk

Thoughts of helplessness

EIGHT OF SWORDS

Interference

Trapped

Frozen by doubtful thoughts

Cannot see the full picture

Over-intellectualizes
this issue

Someone trying to
control you

Someone or something
trying to hide something
from you

Defeat

Self restricted

Refusing to see options

Refusing to believe you
have value

NINE OF SWORDS

Self cruelty

Sleepless nights

Lost passion

Feeling like you have been
 stabbed in the back

Overcome with sadness

Promise of new life

Suspicion

Nightmares

Regrets

Insecurity

Depression

Delays

Pining

Obsession

TEN OF SWORDS

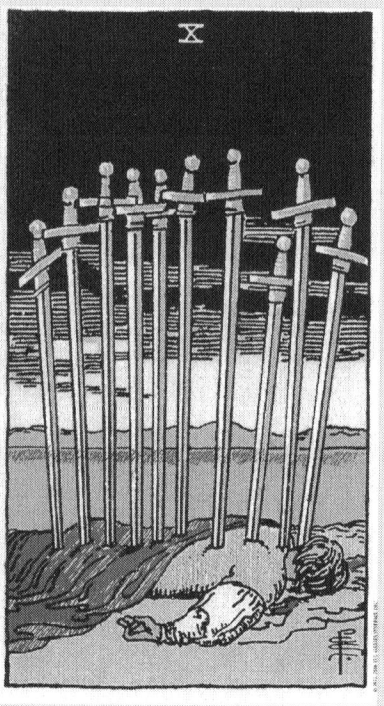

Ruin

Frozen by your own thoughts

Stabbed in the back

Self-abusive thoughts

Overwhelmed

Stuck in a situation where
no one supports your ideas
and projects

Beating a dead horse

Depression

This situation is finished

Time to move forward

Taking a trip over water

Making excuses

PAGE OF SWORDS

Need feedback

New ideas

Earth

Communications

Inability to use creativity

Commitment

Reread the contract

Do not be afraid to ask questions

Someone who is: Intelligent, Perceptive, High Energy, Articulate, A quick thinker, A young man

KNIGHT OF SWORDS

Rushing toward something

Running away from something

An angry person

Victory is not assured at this moment

High action and energy

Fighting for a cause

Saving the day

Social activities

Beating a deadline

Something is going to suddenly happen

Consider timing when considering a plan of action

Take time to have fun

QUEEN OF SWORDS

Gain through courage
Someone who is: A
    trailblazer, A no-nonsense
    person, Intelligent,
    Independent, Determined,
    Pioneering, Empowering
    to others, A heavy-handed
    task master if not evolved

KING OF SWORDS

KING of SWORDS.

In the wilderness

Fairness

Going to receive positive
  information

Ruling in your favor

Promoting your ideas

Someone who is: An
  intellectual, An authority
  figure, Wise, Alone
  and has few friends,
  Analytical, Articulate

THE SUIT OF WANDS

Themes in the Suit of Wands:
South • Fire • Intuition • Spirituality • Perception
Passions • Ambitions • Business • Movement
Midday • Youth • Male

ACE OF WANDS

Reexamining your core
beliefs

Practical ideas

Pure awareness

Recognizing and trusting
intuition

Trusting yourself/
Trustworthiness

Authenticity

Community

Raw high energy

Birthing a new project

Beginnings

Business

Starting a family

Invention

TWO OF WANDS

Dominion

Clear vision

Resourcefulness

Vitality

Enterprise

Work and planning
  bears fruit

Determined

Restored to wholeness

Mindfulness

Boldness

Asking: What is my
  desire or my motivation
  regarding this plan?

Mutual benefit

Commitment

No second guessing

THREE OF WANDS

Virtue

Broadening horizons

Making an educated
decision

Optimism

Distributing resources

Speculation

Launching a new idea

Exploration

Expansion

Educated decisions

Taking the initiative

Distributing resources

Negotiations

FOUR OF WANDS

Completion

Virtue

Vigilance rewarded

Solid foundation

Strong alliances

Peace

Contentment

Gratitude

Well-being

Good friends support
  your work

Celebration/Celebrating
  your relationships

Receiving a raise

FIVE OF WANDS

Playful competition

Possible strife

Fighting over control

Overcoming an obstacle

Legal conflicts

Travel delays

Defensiveness

Creative disputes

Everyone thinks they are right and no one wants to give up their positions

Fighting with self

Passion

Lack of structure

SIX OF WANDS

Victory

Enterprise

Mental leadership qualities

Good news

Victory has already been
achieved

Advancements especially
in the arts or sciences

Celebrating achievements

Be proud of yourself

Helpful friends are on
their way

SEVEN OF WANDS

Taking a stand

Guarding your dreams from predators

Conviction in the face of overwhelming odds

Determination

Victory

Courage

Creative thinking

Feeling on the edge

Being aware of your capabilities in overcoming strife

Not compromising your values

Moving in a new direction

EIGHT OF WANDS

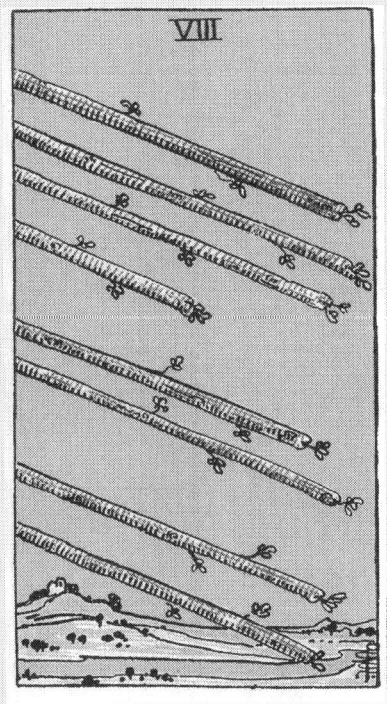

Swiftness

Unexpected assistance

A very busy person

Keep up with everyone

A relationship is moving
quickly

Travel

Positive words create
positive growth

New job

More projects are coming
your way

Work

Action

NINE OF WANDS

Strength
Battered but victorious
Defending yourself
Protect yourself
Stronger and wiser
Clarity and objectivity
Bringing light onto a
    situation

Waking up
The final fight before the
    last issue is solved
The last piece of
    information
Challenges push us forward
Wounded but still standing
You will prevail

TEN OF WANDS

Oppression

Handling a burden

Hard worker

Dependable

Strength

Over-burdened

Back pain

Letting go

Aggressive energies

Resistance to creativity

Doing other people's work
  for them

Completing your work

Not spending enough time
  with your partner

PAGE OF WANDS

Enthusiasm

Acclaim

Encouragement

Messenger bringing
  good news

A love letter is coming

What you have been waiting
  for is arriving

New beginning

A social card

Following your passions

The first spark of an idea

A person with youthful
  energy

KNIGHT OF WANDS

The winds of positive change

Now is the time for travel or moving

Learning from the person that is most unlike you

Do not judge a book by its cover

Challenging yourself to approach issues differently just to see how many things can be learned

A person who is: High energy, Motivated, Artistic, Playful, Loyal

QUEEN OF WANDS

Leaving a mark on society

A person who is: Warm-hearted, Intelligent, Self-made, Idealistic, A teacher, Encouraging and stimulating to others, Empathetic, Creative, Independent, A good manager

KING OF WANDS

Being the change

Someone giving you a hand up

Long-term relationship

A person who is: Playful, Intellectual, Good at keeping the mood light, An older male, A strong communicator, Generous, Kind, Concise, Organized, Positive, Open-minded, A mentor

MAJOR ARCANA

The Major Arcana are the twenty-two remaining cards in the Tarot deck after the suit cards. Commonly called Trumps, the Major Arcana represent ways that you can use your gifts and resources to create success in your life. The Major Arcana tell the story of the universe as well as your own personal story. A good way to look at the Major Arcana is to consider each card as a different lens through which to view your life.

0 - THE FOOL

Great Spirit

Seeker

Genie

Innocence

Human/Dreamer/Hero

Traveler through the story

Seed/Beginnings

Journeys

Joy/Carefree

Folly

Transcendence

Ready to embrace life

The Abyss

1 - THE MAGICIAN

Shaman
Sorcerer
Wizard
Resourcefulness
Flexibility
Charm
The Adept
The first spark of an idea

Cleverness
Fully equipped with all tools
All tools from the Tarot
    deck are yours
You have no beginning and
    no end
As above so below

2 - THE HIGH PRIESTESS

Isis

The Delphi Oracle

Goddess

Intuition

Observation

Wisdom

Future

Magic

Personal understanding
of the Tarot

Adaptability

Silence

Introspection

Reflection

Idea fully developed

Clarity

Moving past the veil

3 - THE EMPRESS

Venus

Earth Mother

Moon

Birth

Nurturing

New ventures

Creative process

Labor pains

Fertility

Sensuality

One who instills confidence
in others

A beneficial influence

Beauty

Effort

Star energy

4 - THE EMPEROR

Sun

King Arthur and the
   Holy Grail

Leaders

Aries

Hercules

Borealis

Fatherhood

Rules

Foundation

Leadership

Intellect

Responsibility

Doing things by the book

Facilitator

Pioneer

5 - THE HIEROPHANT

Buddha

Zeus

Kronos

The Pope

Taurus

High priest

Religion

Advance

Sacred manifestation

Knowledge

Spiritual search

Teaching

Tradition

Mediator

Inner guide

Inspiration

Counselor

6 - THE LOVERS

Yin/Yang

Sun/Moon

Anima and Animus

Gemini

The conscious (male) and
the subconscious mind
(female)

Harmony

Sacred marriage

Relationships

Love

Change

A catalyst

Opposition

Duality

Release your potential

The Explorer	Desire
Helios	Control
Transportation	Courage
Cancer	Finding Your Stride
Victory	Rescue
Ambition	Stuck
Progression	Illusion
Non-movement	

8 - STRENGTH

Bastet

Sekhmet

Fortuna

Leo

Courage

Strength of will

Kindness

Conviction

Empathy

Healing

Inner strength

Understanding

Integration

Infinity

Power through gentleness

9 - THE HERMIT

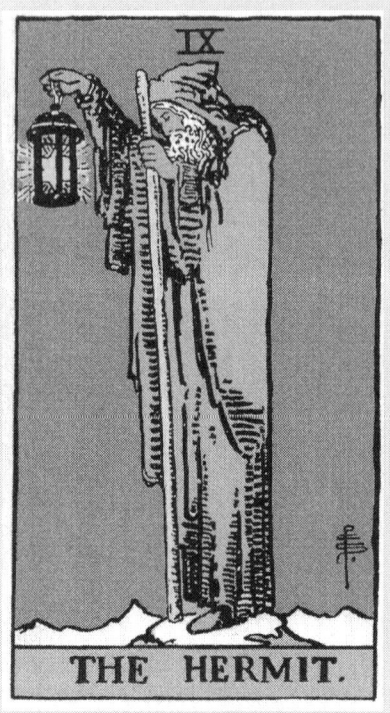

Pilgrim	Harvester
Sage	Solitude
Philosopher	Showing others the light
Virgo	Guidance
Illumination	Helping
Introspection	Prudence
Seeker	Teaching
Herdsman	Star

10 - THE WHEEL OF FORTUNE

Chakras

Medicine wheel

Compass

Destiny

Chance

Movement

Free will

Choice or moral compass

Gambling

The Four Seasons
    and Life Cycles

Good fortune

Change

Breakthrough

Evolution

11 - JUSTICE

Maat

Titaness

Themis

Libra

Law and Justice

Equality

Decisiveness

Decision-making

Non-discrimination

Adjustment

Objectivity

Fairness

Cause and Effect

Paying or receiving a
settlement

Measure your words

Truth will prevail

12 - THE HANGED MAN

Odin	Is your life upside-down?
Thoth	Surrender
Neptune	Mystical experience
Poseidon	Sacrifice
Spiritual breakthrough	Meditation
Initiation	New perspective
Enlightenment	Time to be still
Re-evaluation	Duty

13 - DEATH

Phoenix

Lotus

Butterfly

Reaper

Scorpio

Release

Transformation

Change

Metamorphosis

Rebirth

Death of a project or dream

Endings

New beginnings

Turning over a new leaf

Being prepared

14 - TEMPERANCE

Philosopher's Stone

Artemis

Symbolist

Sphinx

Sagittarius

Integration

Combination

Moderation

Alchemy

Mixed polarities

Testing

Temperance

Adapting

Flexible

Art

One foot in both worlds

15 - THE DEVIL/PAN

Vista	Dealing with your shadows
Satyr	Feeling controlled
Bacchus/Dionysus	Self-made bondage
Capricorn	Unhealthy dependence
Temptation	Only focused on physicality
Endurance	Scapegoating
Restricted	Pessimism
Take off your shackles	Materialism

16 - THE TOWER

Citadel

Furnaces

Deconstruction

Purification

A different approach creates
a different outcome

Opportunity to rebuild

Crumbling falsehoods

Destruction of Ego

Turmoil

Sudden realization

Release of inner fears

Regaining control

The situation is not as bad
as it appears

Time to move

Sudden trouble

17 - THE STAR

Recognition

Orion

Pleiades

Aquarius

Renewal

Healing

New opportunities

Higher awareness

Open-minded

Optimism

Release

Letting go of past hurts

Recuperation

Self-esteem does not depend
on another

Hope returns

18 - THE MOON

Anubis

Luna

Soma

Hathor

Pisces

Illusion

Choice

Passage

A long road ahead

Secrets

Intuition

Only half the story is
being told

Confusion

Instinct

Star moving on your path

There is a clear road to your
destination

19 - THE SUN

The Eye of Ra	Growth
Siva	Rejuvenation
Osiris	Vitality
Sunflowers	Joy
Realization	Learning through play
Enlightenment	Success
Thriving	Having fun as a spiritual concept
Health	
Inner child	Collaboration

20 - JUDGEMENT

Aeon

Pluto

Nuit

Prometheus

Rebirth

Evolution

Transcendence

Freedom from limitations

Spiritual calling

Detaching from materialism, Not entombed any more, Returning to the stars, Self-actualization, Good judgement through observation, it is you who judges your life, Realizing there is no death only transmutation

21 - THE WORLD

The Universe, Nirvana

Global consciousness

Returning to zero

Cosmic egg

Creation, New beginnings

Cosmic dance, Planets

Cycles

Completion

Success

Understanding

Unity, Integration

Victory

Deliberate incarnation

Fixed signs of the Zodiac: Leo, Taurus, Scorpio, and Aquarius

Manifestation

Eternity, Expansion

Liberty through self-actualization

⌒ 2 ⌒

The Key Set Method
of Reading Tarot

Leonardo da Vinci wrote in Notebooks:
"It should not be hard for you to stop sometimes
and look into the stains of walls, or ashes of a fire,
or clouds, or mud or like places in which…
you may find really marvelous ideas."

—C. G. Jung, Man and His Symbols

Key Discovery

When I began studying the symbols in the Rider-Waite-
Smith Tarot deck, I began to notice similarities in the
illustrations. Before I continue, let me talk a little about
the deck. Arthur Edward Waite was a member of the
Hermetic Golden Dawn tradition who commissioned a
talented illustrator and storyteller named Pamela Colman Smith to draw at least seventy-eight cards to form a
new Tarot deck based on the Golden Dawn metaphysical
tradition. Though some believe Smith took all her direction from Waite, she also drew from her own wealth of
knowledge regarding the Tarot. Pamela's drawings were

based on the French Marseille deck and the Sola-Busca deck, created in 1491 in Italy, as well as Papus's (Gerard Encausse) 1892 book *Tarot of the Bohemians*. The deck was then published in 1909 by Rider and Son Publishing in London. The deck could be purchased on its own, or with a simple instruction book written by Waite, entitled *The Key to the Tarot: Being Fragments of a Secret Tradition Under the Veil of Divination*. The publication of the Rider-Waite-Smith deck and Waite's book caused the Tarot to finally be popular among the masses. Waite eventually seceded from the Hermetic branch and created a Golden Dawn branch based on Rosicrucian-Christianity/Roman Catholicism and Smith joined his new group. It was after Waite came upon several old manuscripts discussing the Tarot that he instructed Smith what to draw though some believe Smith added her knowledge of the Tarot as well to some of the Minor Arcana. Waite utilized his metaphysical teachings from the Golden Dawn, the information given to him, and the cards he possessed that had mystical wisdom on them through drawings. Waite would never reveal what the symbols meant because he gave an oath of secrecy; however all the clues are there in each card for anyone who desires to study the Tarot. In addition according to Mary Greer, the court cards are based on one of the Golden Dawn founder's designs based on the photographic post cards called the "cabinet cards," adding to the credence that the Golden Dawn had a big influence on the Rider-Waite-Smith deck. Adding pictures to the Minor Arcana makes it much easier to interpret the cards. Both Smith's and Waite's influences are clearly seen in the symbols in their deck.

As I began to dig deeper into the symbols, I quickly noticed that the columns found in the Death card and

Moon card were the same. I then noticed that the energies for the Death and Moon card, are *solution energies*; that is to say that both of these cards symbolize solutions. So if they are solutions, then what is the question? Then I realized through the discovery of the keys that the question becomes the answer, or rather, within every problem the answer can be found. Then what popped out next was the long red feather found on the Fool's card, which was also repeated on the Knight of Swords, the Death card, and the Sun card. When I discovered the first pairing of what I now call "keys" (meaning a specific symbol), a whole new world of reading the Tarot opened for me, and from there I identified twenty-nine sets of keys that clearly reveal obvious solutions. I worked with them for several years with students. I quickly saw how easy it was to define an issue and identify solutions for my future by using these similarities between cards. These became the Tarot "keys" for the Discovery Path; and I began teaching the keys to students and friends.

It may be helpful to think of the Tarot as a series of keys that unlock our memory, revealing answers and missions that are unique to us. The "key" concept is introduced through the Hierophant and the first six cards. Within the Major Arcana are found all the tools and powers residing inside us. One of the major concepts in the Rider-Waite-Smith deck can be found in the Hierophant card: the concept of dualism. The concept of dualism, or pairing, encourages us to pair the cards, then go beyond that pairing and see that there are many of the same objects throughout the deck. For example, the Hierophant card shows roses and lilies, and there are many other cards that depict roses and lilies that can then be paired with the Hierophant to reveal additional meaning. Other examples of pairing or dualism you can see in the deck include two columns, two priests, two sets of suspenders, two rows of a checkerboard pattern, etc.

The first six cards of the Major Arcana reveal the tools and powers residing in us: the Magician, the High Priestess, the Empress, the Emperor, the Hierophant, and the Lovers. The Magician lays out all his tools on top of his altar, and he shows he is eternal by the infinity symbol over his head and the snake eating his own tail around his waist. He holds one hand toward the heavens and the other hand toward the ground, reflecting the saying, "As above so below." Moving on to the High Priestess, she is holding the book of the Taro; her powers come from the moon and the ocean behind her, and she sits in the temple of Solomon wearing the equal-sided cross which represents many traditions. Next the Empress depicts humans as creators; she is pregnant and sits on a casual chair. Her power comes from being female, which is emphasized by the female symbol sitting next to her. She is wearing a crown made of stars and her field is ready for harvesting. The Emperor shows his power through animal teachings and holding an Isis symbol: the sacred ankh. Then we have the Hierophant, who reveals his power through spirituality. He possesses the keen understanding that he has both a shadow side and a light side and knows how to teach about the light. The Hierophant knows there are barriers at times, yet he also knows how to walk through the storm. The sixth card is the Lovers, which reveals that all our tools and all our powers are found inside us and that Source is always with us giving us strength. Now of course there are many more symbols in each of these cards. I only gave enough examples to show that the first six cards prepare you by revealing that you are completely equipped to take this journey and that you are not here to *become* great; you are here because you are *already* great.

A key set is made up of all the cards that have at least one symbol in common. The keys are expressing that these cards belong together by giving them a symbol in common. Examples: Every card scene that has a path is part of a single key set. Every card in the deck that shows feathers is part of a single category or key set.

Key Sets

Now you have familiarized yourself with the general meanings of the Tarot. Please remember that these are general meanings, and you are not meant to memorize them, just use them for inspiration in terms of telling a story with the cards. If you have a difficult time telling a story, just describe what you see in the pictures on the cards. By describing what you see, you can be guided to the solutions to your questions. For some individuals this will take practice. It is worth it because this process pushes you forward to the solutions for your issues or goals.

Next take out your original Rider-Waite-Smith deck again and begin hunting for several of the key sets to get yourself familiar with a few of the sets for now. To repeat, key sets are a collection of the same symbol that is repeated through the deck; an example of a key set is all the cards that have birds in the scenery or all cards that show water and so on. Why are they important? Key sets help seekers focus on just one symbol at a time and evaluate how that one symbol shows up in different scenes in the deck. They are important because they help you find the answer to your situation through one symbol. In the coming pages I will present step-by-step instructions for you.

Remember, key sets have at least one symbol in common. Below is the Discovery Tarot Path key set list.

First, however, here is an illustrated example of key set # 14, which is a small key set and holds the checkerboard pattern. This key set includes

Three of Wands

Ten of Pentacles

Queen of Wands

The Hierophant

Discovery Tarot Path Key Sets

1. Feathers
2. Flowers
3. Horses
4. Animals
5. Water
6. Mountains
7. Pyramid Mountains
8. Crowns
9. Houses
10. Hidden Faces
11. Boundaries or Walls
12. Infinity Signs
13. Paths
14. Checkerboard Pattern
15. Blindfold or Bindings
16. Moon
17. Sun
18. Stars
19. Cliffs
20. Ships/Boats
21. Vines
22. Nudity
23. Columns
24. Things or Beings out of place or drawn out of perspective or not seen in our normal physical realm
25. Wands
26. Pentacles
27. Cups
28. Swords
29. Crossings

Key Sets' Corresponding Cards

(1) Feathers

26 Cards

King of Swords	Two of Cups
Queen of Swords	The Fool
Knight of Swords	Knight of Wands
Page of Swords	Page of Wands
Queen of Pentacles	The World
Knight of Pentacles	The Star
Page of Pentacles	Judgement
Nine of Pentacles	Temperance
Six of Pentacles	Death
Ace of Cups	Wheel of Fortune
Knight of Cups	The Chariot
Page of Cups	The Lovers
Nine of Cups	The Sun

(2) Flowers

22 Cards

Ace of Cups	Nine of Swords
Queen of Cups	Queen of Wands
Page of Cups	Four of Wands
Six of Cups	Two of Wands
Two of Cups	Death
Queen of Pentacles	The Star
Ace of Pentacles	Strength
Page of Pentacles	The Hierophant
Nine of Pentacles	The Magician

The Sun

The Empress

The Fool

Temperance

(3) Horses

7 Cards

Knight of Cups

Knight of Pentacles

Knight of Swords

Knight of Wands

Six of Wands

The Sun

Death

(4) Animals

33 Cards

King of Wands: Lizard and Lion

Queen of Wands: Cat and Lions

Knight of Wands: Lizards

Page of Wands: Lizard

Six of Wands: White Horse

Ace of Cups: White Dove

King of Cups: Fish

Queen of Cups: Mer-children

Knight of Cups: Fish and White Horse

Page of Cups: Fish

Seven of Cups: Baby Dragon and Snake

Two of Cups: Red-winged Lion

King of Swords: Butterflies and Birds

Queen of Swords: Winged Child, Butterflies and a Bird

Knight of Swords: Butterflies and Birds

Page of Swords: Birds

King of Pentacles: Bulls

Queen of Pentacles: Rabbit

Knight of Pentacles: A Black Horse

Ten of Pentacles: Two White Dogs

Nine of Pentacles: A Trained Falcon and Snail

The Fool: White Dog

The Lovers: The Winged Being

The Emperor: Rams

Wheel of Fortune: Winged Being, Winged Eagle, Winged Bull, Winged Lion, Snake, Sphinx, and Red-Humanlike Being

The Chariot: One Female Sphinx and One Male Sphinx

Strength: Lion

Death: White Horse

The Moon: Two Dogs and a Lobster

The Star: A Long-Peaked Bird

The Devil (Optional): Ram and Humanlike Winged Being

The Sun: White Horse

The World: Eagle, Bull, and Lion

(5) Water

35 Cards

Ace of Cups

Queen of Pentacles

Five of Pentacles

Two of Pentacles

Queen of Swords

Page of Swords

Ten of Swords

Eight of Swords

Six of Swords

Five of Swords

Two of Swords

King of Cups

Queen of Cups

Knight of Cups

Page of Cups

Ten of Cups

Eight of Cups

Five of Cups

Ace of Wands

Eight of Wands

Seven of Wands

Three of Wands

Two of Wands

Judgement

The Tower   The Hermit
The Star   The Empress
The Moon   The Fool
Death   The High Priestess
Temperance   Emperor
The Chariot

(6) Mountains

30 Cards

Queen of Cups   Knight of Wands
Knight of Cups   Page of Wands
Ace of Swords   Nine of Wands
Page of Swords   Seven of Wands
Ten of Swords   Three of Wands
Eight of Swords   Two of Wands
Seven of Swords   The Fool
Ace of Pentacles   Strength
King of Pentacles   The Lovers
Queen of Pentacles   The Emperor
Page of Pentacles   The Tower
Nine of Pentacles   The Star
Seven of Pentacles   The Moon
Ace of Wands   Temperance
Queen of Wands   Death

(7) Pyramid Mountains

3 Cards

The Lovers   Page of Wands
Knight of Wands

(8) Crowns

28 Cards

King of Pentacles	Two of Cups
Queen of Pentacles	Temperance
Four of Pentacles	The High Priestess
King of Wands	The Fool
Queen of Wands	The Magician
Six of Wands	The Hierophant
Four of Wands	The Emperor
Three of Wands	The Empress
Ace of Swords	The Chariot
King of Swords	Strength
Queen of Swords	Death
King of Cups	Justice
Queen of Cups	Tower
Seven of Cups	The Sun

(9) Houses

20 Cards

Ace of Wands	Five of Cups
Ten of Wands	Two of Cups
Eight of Wands	King of Pentacles
Four of Wands	Ten of Pentacles
Two of Wands	Nine of Pentacles
Ten of Cups	Eight of Pentacles
Eight of Cups	Six of Pentacles
Six of Cups	Five of Pentacles

Four of Pentacles
Seven of Swords

The Chariot
The Tower

(10) Hidden Faces

15 Cards

Ten of Pentacles
Ten of Cups
Eight of Cups
Seven of Cups
Five of Cups
Three of Cups
Ten of Wands
Five of Wands

Three of Wands
Ten of Swords
Nine of Swords
Six of Swords
Five of Swords
Judgement
The Hierophant

(11) Boundaries or Walls

12 Cards

Ace of Pentacles
King of Pentacles
Ten of Pentacles
Nine of Pentacles
Eight of Pentacles
Nine of Wands

Six of Swords
Four of Wands
Two of Wands
Nine of Cups
The Chariot
The Sun

(12) Infinity Signs

4 Cards

Two of Pentacles
The World

Strength
The Magician

(13) Paths

5 Cards

Ace of Pentacles Temperance
Eight of Pentacles The Moon
Two of Wands

(14) Checkerboard Pattern

4 Cards

Three of Wands Queen of Wands
Ten of Pentacles The Hierophant

(15) Bindfold or Bindings

6 Cards

Eight of Swords Nine of Wands
Two of Swords The Hanged Man
Five of Pentacles The Devil

(16) Moon

4 Cards

Two of Swords The Moon
Eight of Cups The High Priestess

(17) Sun

6 Cards

The Fool Death
The Lovers The Hanged Man
Temperance The Sun

(18) Stars

19 Cards

Ace of Pentacles	Four of Pentacles
King of Pentacles	Three of Pentacles
Queen of Pentacles	Two of Pentacles
Knight of Pentacles	The Magician
Ten of Pentacles	The Empress
Nine of Pentacles	The Hermit
Eight of Pentacles	The Chariot
Seven of Pentacles	The Star
Six of Pentacles	The Devil
Five of Pentacles	

(19) Cliffs

8 Cards

King of Swords	Three of Wands
Queen of Cups	The Tower
Knight of Cups	Death
Seven of Wands	The Fool

(20) Ships/Boats

5 Cards

Six of Swords	Two of Pentacles
King of Cups	Death
Three of Wands	

(21) Vines

7 Cards

King of Pentacles

Queen of Pentacles

Ten of Pentacles

Nine of Pentacles

Seven of Pentacles

Four of Wands

Three of Cups

(22) Nudity

6 Cards

The World

Judgement

The Sun

The Devil

The Star

The Lovers

(23) Columns

6 Cards

Three of Pentacles

The Moon

Justice

The Hierophant

The High Priestess

Death

(24) Objects Out of Place or Supernatural Beings

23 Cards

Ace of Wands

Ace of Pentacles

Seven of Pentacles

Six of Pentacles

Ace of Cups

King of Cups

Ten of Cups

Seven of Cups

Four of Cups

Two of Cups

Ace of Swords

Three of Swords

The Lovers

Wheel of Fortune

The Chariot

Temperance

Death

The Tower

The Devil

The Sun

The Moon

Judgement

The World

(25) Wands

21 Cards

Ace of Wands

King of Wands

Queen of Wands

Knight of Wands

Ten of Wands

Nine of Wands

Eight of Wands

Seven of Wands

Six of Wands

Five of Wands

Four of Wands

Three of Wands

Two of Wands

The Magician

The Hierophant

The Emperor

The Empress

The Chariot

The World

King of Cups

King of Pentacles

(26) Pentacles

15 Cards

Ace of Pentacles

King of Pentacles

Queen of Pentacles

Knight of Pentacles

Ten of Pentacles

Nine of Pentacles

Eight of Pentacles

Seven of Pentacles

Six of Pentacles

Five of Pentacles

Four of Pentacles

Three of Pentacles

Two of Pentacles

Magician

Devil

(27) Cups

15 Cards

Ace of Cups	Six of Cups
King of Cups	Five of Cups
Queen of Cups	Four of Cups
Knight of Cups	Three of Cups
Ten of Cups	Two of Cups
Nine of Cups	Magician
Eight of Cups	Temperance
Seven of Cups	

(28) Swords

16 Cards

Ace of Swords	Six of Swords
King of Swords	Five of Swords
Queen of Swords	Four of Swords
Knight of Swords	Three of Swords
Ten of Swords	Two of Swords
Nine of Swords	Justice
Eight of Swords	Wheel of Fortune
Seven of Swords	Magician

(29) Crossings

8 Cards

The Hierophant	Ten of Wands
Three of Swords	The World
Two of Swords	The Hanged Man
Five of Wands	The Magician

Five Considerations on the Discovery Path

Before you begin a reading, there are five considerations, or reflections, that have to be taken into account when using a key set. These considerations help define and narrow down our issues and their solutions.

Allow yourself to enter a light meditation and enjoy this process. Make it easy: just relax and listen to your answers to the following questions.

Have you ever experienced a dilemma that seems to have no clear solution? The key sets are designed to clearly show you several approaches to a specific issue. The fact is, when we experience problems in our lives, we are the ones who are supposed to solve them if they are our issues. Therefore, the first consideration is: Is this problem ours to solve? If the problem is not ours, we cannot solve it completely. If it *is* our problem, the key set can help guide us to our solution, or at least diminish its effect on our lives. This becomes simple once we learn how to ask our questions and read the key sets within the cards. A key set is communicating through all the symbols in the card scene. The key inside the scene is important as well, yet its main purpose is to let us know these cards belong together to communicate your story.

The second consideration: Is our question specific and concise? If our question is not specific, we will receive a muddled answer when reading our cards. This is why it's important to make sure your question is clear, so that you will also receive a clear answer.

The third consideration: What is influencing us? The influences that are acting on us will be revealed by the key set, which enables us to be able to identify specific solutions to our issue. No generalities, only specific actions to move through our uncomfortable situation.

The fourth consideration: Do we have the will, inclination, and/or energy to solve this issue? Are you ready to leave the issue behind you and enter into full sunlight by moving past the shadow of your issues? It is possible to succeed if that is your desire. Certainly there are individuals who are scared to death of success or do not think they deserve to experience love, peace, or abundance; but for those that have the will to take action, the keys can help them to find the right action to take by identifying the issues at hand.

The fifth consideration requires us to define what success means to us; not someone else's definition, but our own definition. This is one of the most important considerations. If we cannot define success for ourselves, then how will we know when we are successful? To this end, please write down your definition of success; then post it where it is in sight as a reminder. Make this definition short, simple, and changeable (because success might mean something else to you in six months). Examples of a short, simple definition of success may be

- Living in peace

- Inventing something new

- Being helpful regarding the animals of my state

- Being an effective teacher

- Living on a farm to feed the nation

- Making a difference in my community by adding beauty

- Creating a social network so my business may grow

- Growing a garden

- Being ready to be an adventurer

So before examining the Tarot or using the keys, these meditations and considerations give us clarity regarding where to start when we pick up the cards.

The good news is that the keys are all about you. It is you who reads the cards and it is you who determines their meaning in a way that resonates with what is happening in your life. By the end of your self-reading you will know your future because you will have come up with solutions that you have decided to apply to your life. In fact, you already know your future because who do you think is creating it? *You* create your future. Additionally, if you are a professional card reader, you will be able to lead the querents to their answers as well. Anyone can read the keys; you do not need to be a professional or even experienced in the Tarot to receive wisdom.

Remember, when reading the cards, describe what each card's scene is conveying. This means asking: What is shown in the scene (i.e., people, things, animals)? What is happening in the scene? What will happen if the scene continues? What happened before this scene? You will then compare these answers to the definition of success that you wrote previously, or to the problem that has arisen in your life. What is revealed to you through the cards and the keys will help you to come up with more than one solution for your issue that you can then use to take action. You will soon realize that when you begin acting upon an answer, more answers are ultimately revealed. Remember: you do not hold the message; you *are* the message.

Creating the Key Set Deck

I suggest creating a key set deck so that you can use the deck to randomly pull a key from a key list. Creating a key set deck will be beneficial because it will be easier to work with than just having all the key sets on several pages in this book. To make a key set deck, take a stack of index cards (you can also cut cards out of heavy stock paper) and number them 1 through 29. Alternatively, you could also number twenty-nine chips or stones as well. Each numeral on each card/stone corresponds with a key set. It might also be helpful to write the name of each key set on its corresponding card. To use your key set deck, randomly select a card or stone and then go to the list to find all the cards that have that key. This is the set from which you will form your spread. You can of course consciously choose the key set you would like to use for your spread, but sometimes there is just something satisfying in shuffling a key set deck or choosing a stone at random. It is your choice.

The Discovery Tarot Path Process

The Discovery Tarot Path process or the process of reading your own Tarot through the keys consists of a few steps.

- The first step, as stated previously, is to secure an original Rider-Waite-Smith Tarot deck. It is very important that it is not a re-engineered or redrawn because those decks will not hold all the original symbols drawn by Pamela Colman Smith.

- The second step is to create your key set deck as instructed above.

- The third step is to write your issue or question down on a sheet of paper. This way you will be able to refer back to it as you receive solutions through the cards.

- Next, shuffle your key set deck and take the first card off the top. This card you have taken from the top of your key set deck is the key symbol you will remove from your Rider-Waite-Smith deck. Find the key set list within this book and then pull every card that belongs to the key set from your Rider-Waite-Smith deck. For example, let's say you pull the key set "Horses," so you would then remove all the cards that show horses in the original Rider-Waite-Smith deck, which are Knight of Cups, Knight of Pentacles, Knight of Swords, Knight of Wands, Six of Wands, the Sun card, and Death card.

- For the fifth step, once you have pulled all cards within a single key set out of the main deck, you will set the rest of the Rider-Waite-Smith deck aside and consult just the key set deck that you have drawn. In our previous example, your key set deck would only include cards that contain horses. Shuffle the Tarot cards you have pulled and keep your question or issue in mind as you lay the cards out as follows in the sixth step.

- Now place three cards face down in a horizontal row in front of you. Then place the next three cards in a horizontal row above the first row. Lastly place another three cards in a horizontal row above the other two rows. In total there are nine cards on a flat surface. Set aside the remaining key set cards. You should see three horizontal rows in front of you with every card face down. Example:

3rd Row: Tarot Card – Tarot Card – Tarot Card
2nd Row: Tarot Card – Tarot Card – Tarot Card
1st Row: Tarot Card – Tarot Card – Tarot Card

Special note on working with the thirteen small key sets:

A few key sets have just a few cards, so when you draw one of these key sets, go ahead and draw another key set to complete the spread. You will see the keys still operate the same way. Example: you draw numeral 3, which is the horses key set (seven cards), so you then draw another card from your key set deck that indicates the ships key set (five cards). At this point you have a total of twelve cards, which is more than enough to form a spread.

In the seventh step, you will turn each card over right side up and read the cards in any order that you like. You can start on the top row and work your way downward, or you can start at the bottom and work your way up to the top row, or the cards can be read from left to right or right to left.

I prefer starting at the bottom and working my way from left to right and upward.

The bottom row represents what or who is influencing us, i.e., what or who is helping or hindering us.

The middle horizontal row shows what is happening right now within this issue or question.

The top horizontal row is our outcome regarding this issue or question.

Every row has solutions and answers.

Once you have interpreted the nine cards that were laid out, you will then read the story you are living within this day or week. This is your story only; thus each meaning for each symbol must emanate out of your consciousness, your experiences, your culture, your sensibilities. A black bird may mean something completely different to someone from a different country, a different culture, or even just with different memories. Your interpretation is the most valued; your solutions are there inside the Tarot cards. All of the symbols may not come to you at once; it is okay to leave your spread out, untouched, until the answers reveal themselves to you. As you read your spread, it may be a little static or uncomfortable at first; however you will soon experience meanings that flow beautifully from your subconscious self. For myself, in the past there have been times when there may have been a card I could not interpret for that particular day; it just did not fit with the general story. However, the symbol's interpretation would eventually come to mind and I would know that it was the right one. I thought to myself, "Now I understand this card after moving through my day, I will now learn this lesson."

Once you have interpreted how the symbols relate to your story, you are ready to take the willed action conveyed through the story being revealed through the Tarot cards. A willed action means that a person needs to be willing to receive the answer and then willing to take action. You are creating your future by your actions or inactions.

The Universe and your higher-self yearn for you to hear their communications to you every day. No special day needs to be set aside to read your unique story through the Discovery Tarot Path method.

As you can already see, there are several levels to reading the cards this way, but if this is overwhelming, just focus on one thing, one solution. This is the solution that will carry you forward. What is the card depicting? What is the story that is being told? For some individuals at times it may be overwhelming to read a large number of cards, while other times it may seem very comfortable.

The Tarot helps with your missions and dreams. It offers good solutions to a variety of questions and problems. However, one must also take the steps to move out of a situation or into a situation; you can't simply rely on having wisdom from the Universe without putting it to use.

Now if you want to ask another question using the same key set, just reshuffle the same key set and place the cards in three horizontal rows again. Even with just one key set, you can access dozens and dozens of different stories or approaches to move past limitations or expand your consciousness.

Some Notes on Interpreting the Cards

Empowerment is already yours. The Discovery Tarot Path simply helps you to remove the blindfold to see what you already possess one day at a time. The Discovery Tarot Path process is a perfect union between Deity, symbol, Spirit, ancestors, your higher-self, and your lower-self.

The keys reveal a general story about our human condition and what we can do to release these limitations and claim our gifts. The universe speaks to you personally as a type of channeling. Channeling is Spirit speaking through you. After reading your personal stories through the Tarot key sets, you can choose to follow the advice or not. Learning how to move beyond our physical mind is at times difficult, yet every human is capable of taking advantage of the suggestions given by the Tarot.

Once you have the key set spread before you, interpret each card by intuition or explain what you see on the cards all the while keeping your question or issue in mind. If you need to return to the chapter with the cards' general interpretations, read a few words from the interpretations but try to allow them to be a starting place or jumping-off point for your own intuition.

Remember, this is not a science; it is more of an art.

To help you see what an interpretation of the cards may look like, here is an example from my previous sample reading on page 112 involving the checkerboard key set. Remember, you may interpret this set completely differently because you will have a different question you are asking, and a different worldview through which you see the cards.

The question for this specific sample reading is whether the querent should start his own business and whether he has everything he needs to start it right away. Here's how I would interpret the following cards in light of this question:

- **Three of Wands:** Solutions are right in front of your face. You have planted enough seeds and it is now time to harvest what you have planted for years. Identify all your resources. Write your plan down and show it to as many people as possible. Lastly, stop second-guessing yourself.

- **Queen of Wands:** What attitudes does a cat possess and how can you apply them to this issue? If there is someone discouraging you, encourage them with kindness. Create something completely new.

- **The Hierophant:** This card is reminding you of your skills and the power residing in you. Start and maintain every project in peace, though not easy at times.

- **Ten of Pentacles:** Represents a life well lived. Good decisions have already been made, actions have already been taken, or you would not be in this position and place now.

When you have time, study the key sets. Decide in your heart and mind that you will step into a new adventure today, allowing your light to illuminate your community through the keys and through your life.

⇐ 3 ⇒

Symbolism and Interpretation

*As far as we can discern, the sole purpose of
human existence is to kindle a light of meaning in
the darkness of mere being.*

—C. G. Jung

Symbols and Influences

Now is time to look at all the symbols that have now created our personal story. As we read the Tarot to help us
with our day-to-day living, it is also showing us a bigger
picture, the bigger story that is our life. From now on,
you can begin to lovingly tell your own story. What you
are experiencing in your life is your unique story. No one
else is able to assign meaning to it but you. Ask the cards:
"Clarify my experiences so they become light upon the
earth and my path. Give me revelation, give me inspiration and strength, give me insight to release limitations
in my life."

Now completely relax and allow the cards to speak
to you and through you. Believe in yourself; believe and
trust in your own words. Trust yourself. Trusting yourself
is indeed powerful.

Interpreting Your Solutions

Once you have seen the symbols and keys in the spread you have been working with, you have a choice to either interpret each key symbol intuitively or to begin by studying each symbol individually. As an example of this, let us say you drew the flowers key set, and you want to deepen your study by focusing just on the roses. In this case, you would then research the meaning of a rose. The rose shown on one card may have a different meaning than the rose in another card. For instance, you may see a rose passed between two people and interpret it as an exchange between lovers, but if you see a rose lying on a grave, it would have a different meaning. It depends on the story, the question you ask, and the individual asking the question. All of these factors affect the meaning as everyone sees life differently. Thus, it is always imperative to approach your personal readings with an open mind.

Once you have decided what cards you want to study in depth, then consider what the symbols in the cards are doing and what their attitude may be in the context of the rest of the card. The most important interpretation of a symbol or story is yours, because once again this is your history, your culture, your experiences, your Soul, your future. Only your interpretation will unlock your doors. It may feel awkward in the beginning, but as you speak out, the story soon will feel a little shift and each card will come alive and work for you. As you read your cards, remember no one else can live your life better than you. No one can accomplish the things you are accomplishing better than you. You are here in this life to experience and release your limitations for the good of all humanity.

Identifying Solutions in the Key Set Cards

Some people may have difficulty seeing solutions through symbols. In that case, I suggest that you select one of the following scenarios:

- "I cannot find a job in my career choice."

- "I would like a life partner. How can a good individual enter my life?"

- "When I am in a room filled with people, I feel invisible."

- "My boss does not see how hard I work."

Now read each of the following key sets in light of each of the above scenarios and see how many solutions you can identify:

Ships/Boats (Key Set 20)

Six of Swords
King of Cups
Three of Wands
Two of Pentacles
Death

Sun (Key Set 17)

The Fool
The Lovers
Temperance
Death
The Hanged Man
The Sun

Bindfold or Bindings (Key Set 15)

Eight of Swords

Two of Swords

Five of Pentacles

Nine of Wands

The Hanged Man

The Devil

Another way to familiarize yourself with the cards and develop your own interpretations of them is to skip the card spreads in the beginning and, starting with the Fool card, spend time with a single card per week deciding how you will celebrate it. The next week move to the Magician and so forth until you have created a special little experience reflecting the cards' energies and vibrations, remembering success enters through joy. Then essentially add activities to your life taken from the scene on the card if feasible or use the scenes as motivators.

Considering Influences

As you are considering the cards, keep in mind all the influences in your life relating to your question. We all come to the Tarot with influences and different energy levels. If an individual does not take action to move forward, then this is your choice, but remember that you are the one who made the choice. Consider the mountain of influences you bring to the cards, such as past experiences, motives, dreams, family, workplace, friends, and the many other influences that you experience in your everyday life (everything from what you watch on TV to how the weather affects you is an influence)!

Your Sensibilities or Main Personality Traits

Your personality is one of the main mechanisms that cause you to remedy a problem or remain in a problem. Some personalities choose resistance versus allowing, or they choose to be aggressive versus passive, etc. or an individual may be a consummate starter, faithful maintainer, or detailed finisher. A consummate starter is a person who loves to start projects, forever coming up with great ideas, whereas a faithful maintainer comes in and knows how to keep things running smoothly. A detailed finisher instinctively knows and has the skill set to place the finishing or refining touches on a project or business.

Or a person may also be an experience person, an idea person, a material person, a people person, an animal person, an action person, or a nonaction person... to name just a few. These personality traits can all be important to identify when deciphering your solutions. All these personalities see through different lenses, and all equally beneficial.

General Solution Question

Another good practice is to consider the following questions so that your mind begins to automatically think in terms of problem solving instead of creating emphasis on the problem. If you are having trouble deciphering your spread, ask yourself a few questions regarding your situation from the following list:

- Did I express my needs?

- Was I sincerely remorseful?

- Was I honest yet kind?

- Was I sincere?

- Is this really my problem?

- Is this my responsibility?

- Is this my business?

- Did I strive for real connection?

- Did I take care of myself?

- Did I walk away when I was needed?

- Do I need to take a break from this issue?

- Is this situation, place, or person compatible to my sensibilities?

- What am I learning from this issue?

- Was I positive?

- Did I protect my privacy and boundaries?

- Was I open-minded?

- Did I offer a solution?

- Did I keep my word?

- Did I do all I could to remedy the situation?

- Was I grateful?

Activities to Help You Attune to the Tarot Cards

Many of us have been trained to seek information from others regarding how we should live our own lives. Thus some of us may feel we need to automatically ask others, "What does this mean?" when it comes to reading cards. There is nothing wrong in learning about others' interpretations of the symbols in Tarot cards; in fact it is wonderful to hear others' interpretations of our cards in a spread. It is also exciting to read about Tarot. Just remember that this is your life to decide what you think is best, and what you think is pertinent to your life's mission. No matter how insightful others are or how many good books you have read about the Tarot, it is up to you to receive knowledge outside yourself that resonates with you, and to discard anything that does not feel right.

The purpose of the activities below is to help you develop your observational skills, which you can apply to your Tarot readings. There are many people that have worked with the Tarot but do not always notice many of the symbols depicted within each card. These activities are excellent tools to help heighten your focused intent and naturally usher in pure energy.

Tarot Tracing

Tracing is a method that many architects use while studying building and furniture styles. It is performed simply by laying a piece of paper over the design and tracing it through the paper. By the time the architects have meticulously traced a style, they know every line of it.

To apply this activity to the Tarot, use a piece of white paper and tracing paper and trace the picture on the selected Tarot card in pencil.

Once you have completed tracing your first card, you can then keep the tracing or continue to work with it by adding lines in pen, adding color, framing it and hanging it up in your home, or scanning it to your computer to keep indefinitely.

Just like an architect going over a new style of building, by the time you have completed your tracing, you'll be more intimately aware of what is being depicted in the chosen card.

Start a Tarot Group

Starting a Tarot group can provide many opportunities to practice your skills and learn different approaches from other Tarot readers. The group can take turns reading for each other or the entire group can read for one person. This is a wonderful opportunity to share each other's lives in a meaningful way while developing more confidence in your card interpretations. Meeting with a group on a regular basis encourages folks just to relax and enjoy the process instead of worrying that they are not interpreting the cards correctly.

When you get your Tarot group together, you might want to try creating a spirit message circle using the cards. To do so, ask everyone to relax and allow spirit to speak to them. Each person will then say, "I bless these cards for the purpose of speaking to spirit. Only spirits of the light are welcome here. I request our ancestors, our spirit guides, and Deity to speak to us through the Tarot." Now pass around a deck of cards and ask everyone to shuffle it a few times. Once every person has shuffled the deck, then deal three cards from the deck to each person, face down. Ask the group, "Who would like to reveal what spirit is communicating to you or for another person?

Everyone is welcome to share or you can just observe." When a member of the group feels moved to do so, they may turn over either their own cards or someone else's cards and say, "Spirit is saying..." and they will then give their interpretation of the revealed cards. Once you feel the group is finished, say together, "We thank you, Spirit, for sharing your guidance and support. We bid you hail and farewell with a grateful heart."

Altar

Creating an altar can be as simple as placing a single candle on a small table or as ornate as adding statues of gods, ancestor pictures, or incense. The purpose of placing a Tarot card on your altar may be to ask Spirit to show you more about reality through this particular card. Then watch to see how many things will enter your life to teach you about your worldview and the meaning of this particular card. This works because your focus is toward learning about your world through the cards.

Many individuals have different types of altars in their home. They might honor all their ancestors, a personal Deity, or they may have a healing altar where the focus is upon all those that need physical or mental healing. A Tarot altar's focus is enlightenment. It employs the Tarot to help us grow as humans. Because we are magical practitioners, this is one of our main purposes of living: to become better human beings and to partner with the rest of Gaia's children so we may leave this world a better place than when we first found it. A Tarot altar help us learn about our world and how we present our gifts to the world. Both a personal altar and a specific Tarot altar help our focus our intent to become clear and bright so we may know what we are to learn or accomplish.

Sending a Blessing

Each Tarot card expresses a spiritual precept that encourages our soul to thrive. The purpose of a Tarot blessing is to help you to become aware that you are everything within every card. Every card is a blessing to be applied to your life. Instead of seeing the cards as a puzzle, you may begin recognizing that they have a consciousness.

A blessing is sent virtually through a strong, deliberate thought. By believing it to be so, it is. A consistent thought holds powerful energy that changes lives. A blessing is sent virtually by being in partnership with Deity. A Tarot card can help in forming a blessing or prayer energy. A blessing is an affirmation or prayer requesting Deity and the higher-self assist in healing, protecting, encouraging or aiding a person, place, or thing. It can be a thought sent out into the universe or a carefully written note on a sheet of paper placed on an altar or your nightstand.

Below I have included several sample blessings based on the cards but you should feel free to create your own.

Major Arcana Blessings

A Major Arcana Blessing is an uplifting insight applied to you or sent to another through a prayerful thought.

The Fool	May you lead your life expecting the brightest and best things with good supportive fellowship along the way. May your seeking reach the heights of the snowcapped white mountains. May every step you take be filled with generosity and every possibility.
The Magician	Here lies before you all your tools upon your altar while the protection of roses and lilies surround you. You already know you have no beginning or end. The snake girds your waist as a reminder we return again and again just like our words return to us. We begin with what we need in order to travel our short journey, embracing the same wand we held when we last ascended.
The High Priestess	Behold the High Priestess! Her words slice through all deceit and uphold the crown of truth. Your hand pierces through the veil and holds the cup of life. You produce living springs from inside your inner cosmic ocean. As you sit in front of the deep rushing waters, you see the Tarot is your guidance through the lens of the veil.

The Empress	You shall create humans or create a loving home for Earth's creatures. The water falls in quiet ponds around you. You now wear a crown of illuminating stars in remembrance of your origin.
The Emperor	Behold the Emperor! May you walk through fields of gold and amber high mountains. May you live a long life filled with fruit as sweet as your kindness. Though there are times the stream of life seems choked off, nevertheless it supports your every effort. Even when isolation pushes you aside, know that nothing can separate you from your mission. There is nothing you need to prove.
The Hierophant	We sing praises to the Hierophant. The roses and lilies are treasures giving you infinite life, power, and peace from the long past and reminding you that you are the promise. May the brightest blessings forever follow you home now. It is you who holds the keys to your will and life.

The Lovers	This world has tried its best to discredit the concept of love and reduce its effect. We remember that love is the very mechanism that causes the galaxies, holy precepts, and babies to be birthed. We remember how love unleashes our vibrant light upon everything.
The Chariot	The star wand is never far from you. Your crown of stars, star canopy, and veil shall forever cover you. Service is your gift.
Strength	Power is not harming another or starting wars. Power is calming the lion and wearing roses of the field.
The Hermit	You stand at the apex of your power and there are no weapons involved except the star you hold up toward the other waiting stars above.
The Wheel of Fortune	May the Tarot be your moral compass, your turning wheel, and your mighty wings.
Justice	You know what is right for your life. Justice is not about balance. It is about living in harmony.

The Hanged Man	No matter what life delivers you, your peace shall always shine like the morning summer sun. You will continue this work purposefully created to deliver love to the masses.
Death	The morning sun rises in the East reminding you of the brilliant sun residing within you. Everyone lives a physical life until it is time to live a different life. Everyone deserves to live in peace, not in hostility, including self-hostility.
Temperance	You have been tested and have walked through the flames of injustice only to come out of the fire as tempered steel. May clear waters guide you to the highest mountain peaks, your vast imagination.
The Devil	Today you are ready and willing to take part in healing all hearts, beginning with your own. Today you are ready to lay down all that has bound you in your life. Deciding to not be involved with a controlling individual will help you win your free will back.
The Tower	We have grown too big and bright to remain in strife. May the thunderous lightning bolt remove any outgrown precept that has limited your sacred advancement.

The Star	Behold the star! The star is what we are made of. The star is both our destination and our origin, my stellar beauties. We see the same mountain in the distance calling us home, yet first we care for the water and give drink to the flowers.
The Moon	Now you see everything: you see the illusion, you see a dream. It is time to take the path you have formed over a million lives, and to fly beyond the stars.
The Sun	You are the creator of a gift; you are both the giver and the gift. This earth's sun is a mere speck of what is found within you. It is your hand that tills the earth's ground as you shine with your inner sun. Your preconceptions are like walls to be pierced through.
Judgement	Sometimes we forget what we believe. We overcame death long ago. Because we know we are eternal, we celebrate each crossing until we barely notice we are crossing from one life to the next today. We begin to barely notice our own death because the bridge is so short.

The World	The universe is bigger than what we can see or understand. We are returning to zero once again. We have given our lives to arrive here within this time. We produce Deity's love and send it across the globe so that suffering will finally end. We are the engine of awareness. Both hands are filled with two wands sending energy back to the dreamer, the seeker, the fool.

Discovery Path Card Intentions

Setting an intention can help you in discerning a concrete action to take at the end of a reading. To set your intent, decide on your purpose for reading the cards before laying your cards out in your chosen spread. Place all of your focus on a single intention for that reading. Every Discovery Path purpose is action-oriented in that it is designed to help you to actively remedy a situation, untangle a karmic block, or remove yourself from a long-lasting pattern you have lived over and over in your life.

If may help to write down what your intention is before laying out your spread so you do not drift off into other attentions and thoughts. For this specific reading, you will now have both your issue that you are addressing and your intention or desired outcome written down to help you focus.

You may want to keep the spread out where you can see it for a specific period of time—a day, a week, a month, etc.—to help refocus you toward your intention as you take specific action to achieve your goal.

In the end of course it is you who changes, which in turn changes everything around you. We create our life by our actions—even doing nothing is still doing something. In the beginning pushing yourself to come up with several solutions can be difficult. Make sure the solutions are specific in nature. For example, saying, "I'll just ride this through until people are nice to me" is not specific enough. If anything, this statement is conveying, "I will do nothing until they stop hurting me." A better intention, one that specifies a concrete action, may be, "When this group of people start verbally pushing me around, I will say I need to leave because I need to meet with some friends," or "I will change the conversation, and if they do not pick up on the hint, then I will leave the vicinity." These are just two small suggestions for an individual who is dealing with unkind individuals. The main point is that these suggestions are action-oriented and specific.

Communicating with Your Karmic Teachers' Intent

Communicating with your Karmic teachers will inform you what your Karmic issues are within this life, a past life, or future life. Lay out your cards in the same manner and read cards from the top row from left to right. Write down on a sheet of paper, "What are my Karmic lessons?"

Identifying an Egregore

An egregore is a thought form or a well-developed thought that takes on a life of its own. An egregore is sometimes referred to as a group mind or a hive mind. When a group is working together, they come into synchronization for the good of an important project. Countries or separate locations within a country may have different egregores presenting themselves all differently. It can be directed to help others to be in sync with each other. An egregore embodies the purposes and ideals of the group.

The word egregore comes from the Greek and means "watcher." Once most individuals find out they are part of a thought form or hive mind, they are happy because it satisfies them at a deeper level.

If you find you are attached to a harmful egregore, you will instantly know this and want to move away from this influence unless you enjoy drama in your life.

Are you attached to an egregore? If you are, are you happy being attached to this thought form? You can consult the Tarot to find out if you are attached to an egregore, what kind of egregore it is, and how to release it if you wish.

To identify these thought forms, lay and read the cards as you normally would, allowing them to communicate to you. Keep in mind your intention to identify egregores or hive mind patterns and ask for solutions on how to dissolve them if that is what you wish to do.

In the end, every sustained thought you have in your life has proven that you are on this planet to be part of a good collective work to help maintain and evolve this world. Every storm and trial you have experienced has only proven your Source-given strength.

≈ 4 ≈

The Fool's Journey

I am not what happened to me,
I am what I choose to become.

—C. G. Jung

The Discovery Tarot Path, as well as every living thing, reveals your ever-expanding story. The animals, vast fields, and birds flying above us know what fills us with joy, and the cards can help us find our joy. The most important forgotten mysteries on Earth are remembered through the use of symbols. Yet each essential mystery in the distant past has been torn asunder or ignored. Each has been diminished, even trained out of us as the world races on. This has caused some to think that we have fallen asleep. The Tarot helps us reawaken and to turn our mysteries into practical missions in our lives. These essential mysteries have been turned into something to be marginalized or even worse, but they are our life blood to be utilized freely with no false constructs or conditions attached. Because of this, the true measure of a human being has been long forgotten. We have forgotten that we hold the tools to manifest what is important to our life.

The Tarot speaks to us through symbols, saying, "Return to your power of divine love, joy, and perfect peace so that you may continue crossing the bridge you built eons ago." Peace, love, and joy activate universal power, or your universal mission. No sacred power can be complete or rendered useful without equality. It is not what we know that is important; it's who we help through using what we know.

Though beautiful, love is just not romantic love or family love; love at its core is divine in nature and is activated when given away to others.

Joy is just not a laughing matter; divine joy freely flows out of your Soul like the rushing rivers. Receiving joy creates a laser beam for what you are currently co-creating or manifesting. Receiving and giving human joy activate divine joy, which manifests what you need. You do not need to hunt for joy because you already *are* joy.

Peace is not keeping things in balance or keeping quiet; peace is harmony. Divine peace emanates out of ever-expanding consciousness as it floats through love and joy.

It takes courage and strength to walk the magical life. It also takes courage to approach life full throttle, utilizing the power of divine love and knowing that the power found in peace and joy already resides within you. Combined together, these three feelings activate your power and your mystery. We are the mystery. We are the champions we have longed to meet. Wherever you find a rose and lily or any crossing in the Rider-Waite-Smith deck, they are reminders to utilize these tools that belong to you. You are the mystery, you hold the promise, you are eternal, and you live in this physical life because heroes are needed. When you cross over to the other side of the veil, you are just as alive as you are here in this physical form. Whether we are here or have crossed to the other side, we continue to grow, develop, and help others do the same.

The Rider-Waite-Smith Tarot holds hundreds of stories within the Major Arcana alone; your assignment is to find the stories that relate to your life. The following is one Discovery Tarot Path story that can be found inside the Rider-Waite-Smith Major Arcana which helps individuals to see their own story and their own journey.

The Fool's Journey to Self-Meditation

Once upon a time, the Fool entered this world. This Fool is forever willing to experience everything. We see the Fool experiencing life as the grand Seeker as he begins an exciting journey. He begins his journey already as a success. He is already fulfilled. He knows that no matter what experiences, what trials or triumphs he encounters, he will safely return to eternity and to his ancestors. He is confident, never forgetting his powers and promises as he moves through every life and experience at the same time with divine love, joy, and peace as his guiding Source.

He already knows that every issue he faces in life will reveal many lessons and solutions as well as gifts. Once these influences are identified, removed, or diminished enough to see the solution, the Seeker soon remembers it is he who holds the power. Once solutions are found, it is time to move out away from the trials in life, or diminish them by utilizing peaceful joy and powerful divine love. He then moves to the next experience. After learning each life lesson, the Seeker soon returns straight to the World card—to his center, to zero, and to eternity once again to grow and learn there. However, for now he begins a new life.

The Fool is a dreamer and seeker. The Fool is you as you walk through life, learning lessons through self-selected experiences according to your nature and what you desire to learn. The Fool is born with everything he needs; he is not unprepared. He is crowned with laurels signifying success that will be delivered through peace, fertility, and natural abundance, which is also depicted by the pomegranate design on his tunic. He is a spiritual pioneer, and this is reflected by the long red feather worn on his hat. With the sun at his back, he holds a rose. The rose represents that he knows love, life, and light is his power, a union that never passes away. The rose also mirrors secrets and a symbol of balance. The happy white dog is the Seeker's joy, and companion.

Snow is water and water in all forms holds knowledge. Snow reminds us about the knowledge from above. Every card depicts the Fool's walk toward full consciousness, toward new heights and new lessons. This is one of the Seeker's goals: to return to full consciousness and eternity. This too is represented by the mountains. He knows no matter what he experiences the mountains of the Divine are never too far to reach. Every physical life experiences transition. It may appear as though the story has ended, yet in the astral realm we continue to live.

The Fool is ready to step off the mountain and return to the lush green valley below. He closes his eyes for a few moments, and then reopens them, and realizes on doing so that he is now dressed differently and living a different life. He has become the Magician.

As the Seeker becomes the Magician, he sees that he has all the tools he needs to move through life. He is inside the circle that embraces his waist. It is the Ouro-boros belt (a snake eating its own tail) and he wears it to represent the end of his life; he returns to his beginnings, the cycle of life.

The strong Magician presents the staff, pentacle, sword, and cup as he holds his wand aloft in his hand, bringing us again to the World card where the ascending woman holds one wand in each hand. The Magician celebrates choice. Here we see lovely lilies created by the breast milk of Hera. This is the first power introduced into this story; the lily invokes peace and birth. The lily represents the promise that resides in all of us, the most important power of all: that we are eternal beings visiting Earth for a short time to experience the physical world and then return to eternity. Some say the Magician's stance is showing he is acknowledging the old adage, "As above so below." And so the Universe, so the Soul, as within so without. He never forgets that he is eternal with the infinity symbol floating over his head.

It is time to expand and move to the next stage.

The Magician now closes his eyes for a few seconds and opens them to become the magnificent High Priestess, who ushers in strength, sovereignty, and championship among humans. The Seeker's pomegranate shows up again, printed on the veil hiding the vast sea behind her. She holds a book of Tarot stories safely in her lap. She wears three moons on her head representing equality, free-will, and forgiveness. A fourth moon at her feet implies that her foundation is mutable. She holds the powers of all things that are of the night. She empowers you and you empower her.

With one blink of the eye the High Priestess now transforms into the Empress, bringing you the light of the ancient stars.

The Empress is here sitting before you, reminding you that you are also of the light—you are light and you come from the light. You come from the most distant stars. She wears the Seeker's laurel crown and adds a crown of stars. A rushing waterfall is on her left, a vast golden field is in front of her and a forest of mostly evergreens is behind her. Every element on her card radiates security and strength. She is powerful, and she sees your life. She is Venus, the goddess of victory, fertility, and love, and the strength of the female symbol rests at her side. The Empress is pregnant with new life and possibilities. She represents giving birth to new possibilities and proves that nothing is holding you back except sometimes your own philosophies and dogmas.

Soon the Empress is transformed into the Emperor. The Emperor shows that our Souls are timeless. We are as old as the mountains and this man sitting on his solid stone throne, yet the man-made throne cannot compare with the brilliant sky or the slow moving river behind him. Notice how with the first four cards, each personality looks directly at you; however, the Emperor does not—his eyes are diverted. He looks away. He holds a holy ankh in his right hand and a piece of fruit in his left hand. He is resting and preparing for the story ahead of him. This is now the second time the divine mountains, which represent eternity, are seen in the story. The Emperor is the Seeker's strong foundation. The Emperor says, "In barren times see in the vast emptiness all the blessings you hold in your hands." Soon we see the strong Emperor becoming the Hierophant.

The Hierophant repeats what the Magician is conveying, yet this time he or she says, "You are the key. You hold the power through peace and love. It is you who moves the world by your divine peace and divine love. The triple-crowned Hierophant enters now, introducing the precept through the symbol of crossed keys that all of the repeated symbols in the Major Arcana are keys. When combined, keys activate the silver lining or lesson behind every trial and show you how to move forward while giving blessings. As you now see, most of the main keys within this story are in the first five cards. The Hierophant as well as all the cards are humans living many lives. This scene highlights dualism; notice there are two columns, two men before the Hierophant and two keys on the floor, all indicating that blessings and lessons will be delivered in pairs and that life is for blessing others, not just ourselves.

It is now time for the Lovers and the winged being to reveal that all possibilities are yours. You are the winged being visiting this reality as well as a female, flame, male, healing snake, mountain of full consciousness in the distance, and the brilliance of the Sun giving light over everything. We enter this life with nothing except the will to learn more lessons to add to the lessons we learned in previous lives.

We see a female energy ready to take part in this experiment and a male energy willing to be part of this story, ready to combine efforts, joining dominant and recessive energies together equally to create an entirely new energy and sphere between them. This new energy is being tested and forged through the fire, to show you are already strong and wise.

Now enters the Chariot. The winged being from the Lovers card has turned into a strong stout warrior standing in his chariot with his two Sphinxes near a flowing river. The two lovers are now the two Egyptian sphinxes relaxing on green grass. The sphinxes say, "Come with us and consider the riddles we shall present to you." Each riddle or quiz posits a scenario and asks, "If this happens, what will you do?" This is the single question posed to you throughout your life. It is not what happens to you that counts; it is how you handle what happens to you. When a person does something unkind to you that is a part of their path, what you do in return, however, is your path. The Chariot presents a last reminder before the Seeker moves through the challenges to come, saying, "Remember that you are the winged one. Remember that you are the promise. Remember that your home is the stars." The man in the chariot is standing still, holding one of the same wands the woman holds in the World card, proclaiming that your focus points to the energy you are raising and attracting to you.

With the first challenge enters a woman named Strength. Once again, this is you, wearing a holly wreath and an apron made of roses. A young woman dressed in white with the eternity mountain behind her, she lovingly has everything under control. A lion approaches her and she instinctively soothes his aggressiveness with gentleness, thus demonstrating how lasting strength is found in gentleness, not aggression. She is then rewarded with a second crown of infinity.

The young woman now transforms into the Hermit walking on snow at night during the darkness of a new moon. What will the Hermit do in the darkest of nights, i.e., the darkest of situations? This is the challenge, and he answers by capturing a star from the sky and placing it in a lantern just like catching a firefly and placing it in a jar. The star he has captured is now creating a path of light for him where there was none before. He thus walks in safety, and is reminded of his own vastness. He stands in contemplation as if in prayer or meditation. He is open for anything, not hidden away in a cave. "You are the star found in every lantern—found in every sky."

Now we see the Hermit dissolve into the snow-capped mountain and a new scene appears: the Wheel of Fortune. This time we see the winged being return, in fact there are four winged beings. Other previous symbols return; the word Tarot, the lion, the snake, and the sphinx. An eagle also appears for the first time as well as a bull. The beings resting on clouds are all reading books on this card. They are ascended creatures just like the winged being. The creatures attached to the flat disk are embracing Tarot's universal truths. We are all of these creatures as well as the disk. We see the elemental symbols representing water, earth, fire, air, and spirit as well as Hebrew symbols representing the names of God. This disk is a compass. Are you overwhelmed by all the lives you are now living? One life you live by the sword, one life you live as a healer, one life you are a flying being in another reality, four of you are already safely home inside eternity. The Wheel of Fortune also conveys we know how to move through the constellations because we are there as well as here right now—we are in both places; we are capable of being in two places at the same time, in other words bi-location through our imagination. I know this is difficult to grasp, being in two places at the same time or living many lives all at the same time, but nevertheless this is the complex being you are.

Consider the last five cards we've just discussed: the Lovers, the Chariot, the Strength card, the Hermit, and the Wheel of Fortune. How will you apply their experiences to your life? These cards introduced the main methods to vanquish attachments.

With the next five cards the mood begins to sharply shift as Justice shows up. This card reveals that justice can be found with the sword and met through measured balance; justice can be met by passing the two columns' threshold and crossing the purple veil, entering spirituality. Justice can be found through the power of carefully measured words. Justice can be found with the power of the crown or the humility of the simple understated chair in which she or he is sitting; all these are different approaches to justice.

Next we move on to the Hanged Man and the power of channeling or prophecy. Here you find yourself in deep meditation, considering all you have learned up to this point. You understand sacrifice and walk in wisdom and intuition. Mastering divination, you rest in this knowledge and all is well. Your focus is on peace, ascension, and love. The Seeker is well and strong.

Next you see you have become Mr. Death riding on a magnificent white horse. You know this is you as the Seeker because of the long red feather on Death's head. You feel happy informing anyone who desires to hear that death has no hold on anyone or anything. You look around, seeing that every single symbol that represents life is all around you: the same sun rising in the East, the roses, the cliff, the distant eternity mountains from previous cards. You soon notice that there are two individuals listening to your proclamations; they are a clergy member and a small child. You also see how the youngest child comforts the older child dressed in a white gown. She wears a red rose, meaning that she is ready to hear the mysteries that proceed out of Death's mouth. Though the

Rider-Waite-Smith deck interprets this card as mortality, I see the opposite—I see immortality, expansion, and change.

Next you are transformed into the winged being dressed in a white gown with the sun symbol on your forehead and a positive energy symbol on your chest. You are pouring water into water and over water representing that all knowledge is connected, just as all things are connected by water. You see your clear path coming out of the water, moving toward those same distant mountains over which the sun has now completely crested; however, this time you see your crown floating in front of the sun waiting for your return. The royal irises signify the goddess Iris who personifies the rainbow, the one who ushers us across the veil. Irises bring favor upon the earth. We receive a little respite with the Temperance card. You have your white gown and the single red feather is now fully extended into red wings, and the crowned sun and the Fool's mountains are right behind you with a clear path leading you home.

Now you see the evaluation time is here, with the Devil. As before, the Seeker is everything depicted here: the Pan figure; the dominant and recessive energies; the fruit, flame, and chains. Which chains are we willing to break? We are chain breakers. What is the weakest link in our attachments? The pentacle is turned downward, which represents the concept that the deepest spiritual precepts are the ones that lead us to ascension. The pentacle is pouring insight and protection onto the two humans so that nothing stands above them. Pulling down all pedestals is liberating; you bow before no one. You are the winged animal sitting on your perch, finally realizing it is time to release your tools or gifts upon humanity to grant healing to all.

Then you become the Tower, the two humans, the thunder, and the flame. You see everything that has tried to harm you or tried to hinder you now being removed, the last attachments that hung on to you for far too long. Allow anything that needs to be released to be released. Now see the crown returning to cover the tower, see the flames extinguished, see the sun returning; the moon and stars come out to soothe you and to mend you as this building mends. The building begins to glow as white as the snow it is sitting upon. Now you begin to realize you have walked the path to the mountains of the divine and the divine has made sure that everything you didn't need was shaken loose from your foundation.

The last five cards' energies return the Seeker to the theme of transcendence, each card bringing you closer to eternal bliss. Take deep cleansing breaths and allow deity to touch you; allow your ancestors to support you. With each breath go deeper into awareness and space so that all you see are the stars spinning around you. Allow yourself to take in their stunning energy, and be filled with healing and memory. You look around and notice that you are indeed one of the stars. Allow this situation to be enjoyed for a few moments. The Star card ushers in the final preparations for all the wisdom we have collected. We can now return to the water and add to the universe and to humanity. We are stripped of all attachments. Some attachments we were delighted to remove while a few took lifetimes to address. Nevertheless, here you are in all your pureness and power; every star is eagerly bathing you with light before you return to eternity.

The Moon arrives, allowing starlight to shine upon the earth at night. The Moon in turn reflects the light of the Sun. You are now being shown your life in its entirety before you travel to the mountaintop. You see yourself as the stars, as the brown dog, the yellow dog, and as the lobster. You see yourself as the full Moon, pouring her reflected light upon your ancient Soul.

The Sun card remembers when you were a baby and you possessed all the necessary goodness required to help you come back home. You have seen these symbols before: the long red feather and your life companion the white animal that lived with you all your life. The Sun watched over you and made you grow in wisdom and beauty. The Sun supported you every day of your life as you remembered when you were first given your long red feather on your young white horse.

The Judgement card arrives showing you in the sky with your white robes and red wings, proclaiming that this journey is everyone's to take and that death is an illusion. Graves made by human hands cannot hold our spirits; nothing can hold us because we are pure ever-expanding consciousness. There is no us and them. It is our physical condition that makes it seem at times that Deity is far away but she/he is not. Death is nothing but an illusion.

All of us are the Fool, the Seeker traveling many lives. All of us are in every card, every symbol. Notice that in the last five cards clothes are not needed because we all stand before Deity in our full beauty with nothing to hide. No one judges us. We take measure of our experiences. We open our eyes to transcendence; the World.

We are all represented by the woman in the World card: transcending, returning to eternity, returning to Zero to the center of the wheel, still wearing her simple laurel wreath with a red feather woven into her hair.

She helps us remember that we come from the stars and live for a short while in this reality system on earth, celebrating Earth, the Sun, Moon, and all the Stars. All things ascend: humans, animals, and all things found on the mountains live forever. We are found on the mountain; we are one once again with our ancestors.

Every card offers instruction on love and peace. Love is firm, love is gentle. Love is our protective ring that shall forever surround our being.

The World helps us understand that positive aggressive energy builds bridges among nations. Recessive energy moves everything forward with little effort and is endless. Combining both energies creates an infinite circle of energy. Once this great truth is realized by humans utilizing both positive and negative energies as well as male and female energies equally, this planet will catapult to the next evolutionary leap. New powers, new concepts, and new organisms will be birthed and studied while hidden organisms and senses will finally show themselves.

And guess who shows up on the top of the mountain on the edge of the cliff again?

You.

Now whenever you shuffle the cards, you will discover many more story sequences with many more solutions and confirmations, but this meditation shows you the main story thread that flows through the Discovery Tarot Path keys.

The Discovery Tarot Path is here to remind human beings that they are capable of transforming their world. We are equal with all living things. We are equal with everyone from every nation.

You are joy, you are love, you are peace living inside a human body. You are a multidimensional spirit living in a physical body, but your imagination and your dreams never allow you to forget the other worlds and your purpose within each realm

In Conclusion

Joy is the Beginning of Living Life

*Your visions will become clear only when
you can look into your own heart.
Who looks outside, dreams; who
looks inside, awakes.*

—C. G. Jung

As humans we gain access to manifestation when we experience genuine joy. If we find joy through the simple pleasure of the Tarot, we will be opened to all manner of success.

Remember, however, that success depends on our definition of it. True success is ours from the very beginning of our journey. My definition of success is pure joy. We are here to know that we are happiness and this is the power.

Success cannot enter through negativity or sadness. Joy attracts success. The success you define in joy arrives in your life at the right time. Success as defined by others for you may never arrive or may be a sad substitute.

The Tarot cards are meant to be a self-directed counseling tool and a catalyst to joy. The cards remind us that the three great powers within all of us deliver everything in this world. Everything begins and grows by love, joy and peace.

May the Tarot deliver pure joy into your future exclusively designed by your hand.

I hope you will unleash your unique light upon this world. The keys imbue new perspectives and new awareness. We do not perceive our world then respond to its events—quite the opposite. We create the physical world and every event through our senses. We are not outside this creation cycle; we are inside it.

May the radiant light residing within you touch every corner of the world.

Blessed Be.

About the Author

Stephanie Neal has been a student of the Tarot since the early seventies, utilizing the Tarot deck for counseling purposes, which proved to be incredibly successful. Neal went on to teach the Tarot for decades in countless workshops and podcasts. She is the founder of the Discovery Tarot Path, taught within the Seminary Door system of the Correllian tradition, which is a journey utilizing the Tarot to uncover our core beliefs and uniqueness. This book is part of that path.

Neal is a member of the American Tarot Association and has written courses for the Cherry Hill Seminary and Correllian Seminary. She has served as matriarchal joint-head of the Correllian tradition and chairperson for the Correllian Council of Elders since 2015 and invested in office in 2016.

She is the founder of the Correllian Shaman Order, the Sea Priestess path, and the author of the insightful book, *The Untraining of a Sea Priestess: A Practical Journey to Connect with Cosmic Water Wisdom*, also published by Turning Stone Press.

Neal was a panel presenter for the Parliament of World Religions in Salt Lake, Utah, in 2015 and Toronto, Canada, in 2018. She teaches and produces a show called Elder Radio on blogtalkradio, founded The Global Tarot Association, and is currently painting a new Tarot deck for the Tarot world.

Made in the USA
Coppell, TX
31 January 2022

72682781R00106